Christ Alone - The Narrow Way

Men Walking With God on the Narrow Way to Life

Daryl Synstelien

DDS
DDS PUBLISHING

DDS Publishing

Contents

MAPPING THE JOURNEY
The Narrow Way

Dedication

To Those Who Are Part of Me

With love, appreciation, and gratitude,
I dedicate this book to:

***

The two men who love, care, protect, and provide for
those I treasure (my daughters and grandchildren)
Erik and Kyle
The mighty men who have pastored me, and with whom
I have had the privilege to serve alongside as an elder.
The Pastors and Elders
of
Bethel Lutheran Church
Fergus Falls, MN
All the men with whom I have worked, worshiped,
struggled, wept, and laughed through the years.
Yes, *you.*

A MAN NEEDS A MAP

Two Are Better Than One

DDS

DDS PUBLISHING

DDS Publishing

Chapter One

Men Walking Together

On The Narrow Way

[Jesus] began to teach them, saying... "Enter through the narrow gate; for the gate is wide and the way is broad that leads to destruction, and there are many who enter through it. For the gate is small and the way is narrow that leads to life, and there are few who find it." (Matthew 7:13-14)

Two are better than one because they have a good return for their labor. For if either of them falls, the one will lift up his companion. But woe to the one who falls when there is not another to lift him up. (Ecclesiastes 4:9–10)

ALONE—AND FEELING LOST

Tick, tick, tick... the second hand of the wall clock droned on relentlessly. The fly on his desk, buzzing from crumb to crumb, exploring the remains of yesterday's sandwich, was the most interesting part of Ethan's day. Things were quiet at the office today, with upper management at a planning retreat. Ethan dreaded their return on Monday with a list of bright ideas that would pile on the pressure. Ethan remembered a time when he would have eagerly taken on the new challenges. But in recent months, he cared little about his work. He would brood over the meaninglessness of his routine, and daydream about quitting his job and walking away from the daily grind which it had become. Today was one of those days.

Three years ago, Ethan was excited about the opportunities ahead when he received his promotion to sales manager for a sporting goods manufacturer. What an exciting time in his life! He and Alicia were married just five years earlier. He had met Alicia at university and fell in love with her bright smile and soft blue eyes. They married in the fall after graduation and worked hard to save money for a down payment on a comfortable four bedroom, two bath home across town from where Ethan had grown up. The house filled with life when they brought baby Conner home from the hospital seven months later. They named Conner after Ethan's dad. In every way, Ethan and Alicia's lives seemed perfect and wonderful. All of life was bursting with opportunity.

But just after Conner's second birthday, Grandpa Conner died from heart failure. His father's death hit Ethan hard. It was the first death of a close family member that he had experienced. It was unsettling how alone and empty he was. He worked hard to support and help his mom over the months ahead, but she seemed to adapt and move on much easier than Ethan did. That was difficult for him to understand. When he had asked her about it, she explained to Ethan that, yes; it was difficult, but she understood that life was fleeting. She had a firm confidence that because of their mutual faith in Jesus, she would join Ethan's dad for eternity in heaven soon enough.

Of course, Ethan realized that was true. Christianity was fundamental to who he was. As a child, his parents had brought him to church and Sunday school since birth. He fondly recalled the summer kid's club program when, as a 7-year-old, he responded to the teacher's invitation to pray and ask Jesus into his heart. Then, in his teen years, he attended church youth group and looked forward to summer Bible camp each July. After marrying, he and Alicia continued to attend the same church in which his parents had raised him. They agreed in their commitment to belong to the church, and they wanted to raise Conner to know Christ as his savior.

Ethan was certain of his Christian faith, but his dad's death left him feeling numb and helpless. He felt like a boat being wildly tossed around in a stormy ocean. After a few tough months following his dad's death, Alicia suggested he could contact Jonathon Clauson, an elder of the church, for support. Ethan didn't want to talk to anyone about such personal matters, but Alicia persisted. Eventually, Ethan agreed he would reach out to Jonathon for help. Ethan respected and trusted Jonathon as an elder of the church, and it helped to know that Jonathon had been a close friend of Ethan's dad for many years.

Jonathon sounded genuinely happy to hear from Ethan when he called. When Ethan asked if they could talk about things, Jonathon suggested they meet for coffee the next afternoon.

When they met, Ethan described to Jonathon his struggles after his dad's death. He shared about his inner turmoil and the overwhelming anxiety he felt. Jonathon listened to Ethan's concerns and responded to his questions. They reviewed what the Bible teaches about redemption, death, eternity, and heaven.

Jonathon and Ethan met regularly over the next couple of months. They talked at length about the significance of a parent's death on an adult child, and other major transitions in life. Ethan had never considered these things before. Jonathon shared with Ethan his own process of grieving the same loss, but as a close friend and confidant. It was meaningful for Ethan to understand that Jonathon was grieving along with him, and it was encouraging to hear his support and understanding.

Ethan began to understand that a reasonable process of grieving his dad's death was important, but he still had a wife and son who needed his daily leadership, support, and care. This was an important step in gaining renewed purpose and motivation. He looked forward again, not continually focusing on the past's loss.

Over time, Ethan found peace as he accepted his dad's death. The sadness and feelings of loss did not disappear, but he found comfort and strength as Jonathon encouraged and prayed with him each time they met. Jonathon helped him understand even redeemed Christians experience great sorrow and loss as normal parts of earthly life. Recognizing the truth that he was never alone, that God had promised, *"I will never desert you, nor will I ever forsake you,"* [1] was comforting to Ethan. Jonathon's friendship encouraged him, as they opened their lives to each other each time they met. Ethan was grateful the future was becoming brighter, as he planned for his family.

Home life grew busy with an active little boy, and work life intensified with business growth. After several months, Ethan found he often had to postpone or cancel meetings with Jonathon. That was okay since things had improved, and Ethan wasn't stuck in the sorrow of losing his dad. The occasions of meeting with Jonathon decreased in frequency and then ended.

---

1. Hebrews 13:5

Now, sitting here in his office about a year later, Ethan realized he was listless, bored, and unmotivated. It differed from how he struggled after his dad died. It was less emotional and fearful, but similar in some ways. Quite different from being thrown about by stormy seas, today life's waters were flat and still, with no wind in his sails. Ethan had no clear direction or purpose for his life. Twice over the last two months, he had shared his feelings about his job with Alicia, but it was obvious from her response that it scared her to think he might consider quitting his job. How would he provide for his family? Didn't he understand he had a wife and a five-year-old son to care for? Of course, he understood all of that! But how long could he continue without a sense of purpose and meaningful goals?

That evening, after he tucked Conner into bed, Ethan again felt compelled to talk with Alicia about how long and hard the days at work were. He tried to be reassuring that he knew his responsibilities, and he had no intention of jeopardizing their family's care and well-being, but that he also needed to find some direction and purpose for his life. He was missing something central to who he was as a man, and other than finding a different job, he did not know what else that might be.

Alicia listened, working hard to set aside her own fears of financial insecurity. She recognized that she also wanted Ethan to be fulfilled and engaged in work with a meaningful purpose. After some time of listening and contemplating what Ethan was saying, she responded with a thoughtful suggestion. "Ethan, do you remember how much you struggled after your dad died? Do you remember how you just couldn't see any hope or future with your dad gone from your life?"

Ethan nodded.

Alicia went on, "You could not push through that awful time on your own; you needed a friend's help—and Jonathon was that friend. His friendship was helpful for you, and you seemed different and better and even stronger after every time you met and talked with him. He couldn't change the fact that your dad was gone, but talking and praying with him, and learning from scripture together, helped you to see and think about things differently. I wonder, Ethan, do you think it might be helpful to call and talk with him again?"

Alicia is right, Jonathon thought. The voices in my head are not helping me deal with my life at all right now. I need to hear wiser counsel. "Yes, thanks Leesh, that is a great idea. If Dad was still here, that's who I would go talk with. Jonathon was there for me after Dad's death. He cared for me and listened. Just talking with him helped me to understand everything I was going through. Most importantly, he helped me to see and understand the truth in the scripture about what I was going through. Maybe that's what I need again, now. I'll call him."

WALKING TOGETHER

Jonathon agreed to meet Ethan for breakfast early the next Saturday morning. After some light conversation, Ethan thanked Jonathon for taking the time to meet with him again. He didn't hold back, and launched right into describing the feelings of purposelessness with which he had been struggling for some time.

Jonathon listened carefully. He asked Ethan to explain the responsibilities of his job and for details about the goals that were set for his position. Finally, he inquired about Ethan's relationships with his coworkers and supervisors. Ethan had never talked with anyone about his job this thoroughly.

"Well?" asked Ethan. "Is there any hope for me in this job?" He couldn't resist showing a sarcastic smirk.

Jonathon smiled, "Frankly, no. There is no *hope* for you in this job, or any other job. I wonder if you are expecting or wishing for something from your job that it can't provide. If that is the case, then your trouble is not with your job, it's from within you. Even if you got a different job, you may find yourself in the same troubled place down the road. A wise man once said, 'Wherever you go, there you are!'"

Jonathon allowed Ethan time to contemplate this challenging thought. "Ethan, you understand that all hope and truth are only in Christ. Remember how when your dad died, it was as though nothing would ever be okay again for you? We looked to scripture to learn the truth and to understand our hope and confidence are in Christ. Then we worked at destroying the speculation that you would never be safe and feel courageous again in this life. It took some time and discipline, but God's truth is certain and unchanging. We found that as you took your thoughts captive and measured them up against the truth of scripture, you found peace – even within a time of grief. Understanding and applying God's truth in your life, and challenging the lies and false narratives that have become rooted in our minds, is a significant and continuing process. It's a battle in which we need to be alert, and our fight needs to be intentional. Now you are wrestling with thoughts and feelings about the value of the work you do. It's a different group of feelings and thoughts – but very much the same type of issue."

Ethan studied Jonathon's gaze for a moment, and responded, "I don't understand how what you're saying will fix this issue, Jonathon. I can't see how things can get better at this job. But I trust your judgement, and you helped me work through things before. I'm willing to listen, and try almost anything to get out of this hole I'm in at work. I need to get out of it!"

"This is a tough time you're going through, Ethan," Jonathon spoke with understanding. "I have some ideas on how we can tackle this issue. There are some foundational building blocks of truth about which scripture is very clear concerning who you are, how God created you, and God's design for your life in relationship with Him and others. All these things are also true for me, and for every other man. As men, we need to learn, understand, and apply these truths about the knowledge of God from scripture. Then we can measure our thoughts and feelings against God's truth. It's sometimes a hard process, but it is much more successful when two men work through it together."

Jonathon gave Ethan some time to consider this. When he saw Ethan's responsiveness, he proposed they walk together on this journey. He said, "Ethan, I would like us to partner up and commit to spending time together on a regular, ongoing basis. I think you need that, and I know I need that too. This kind of friendship builds up all men (1 Thessalonians 5:11). Their faith is stronger, and they find encouragement and support while facing tough times and struggles (Ecclesiastes 4:9-12). And most importantly, men need to have someone whom they trust to tell them the hard things – to hold them accountable in their commitment to walk in God's ways (Proverbs 27:5-6). You may not know this, but your dad was that partner for me during the last twenty years of his life. He was only a few years older than me, but I saw him as a true mentor and teacher, besides being my closest friend. We bared our souls to each other, studied scripture together, and depended on one another to shoot straight when we needed to hear the hard things."

"Wow!" Ethan exclaimed, "I knew you were great friends, but I didn't realize the depth of your friendship. That's amazing! I didn't even realize that kind of friendship was possible. After Conner was born, Dad and I connected on a more regular basis. We would meet for breakfast or go hiking together sometimes. I would have Conner in the backpack carrier and we would hike up to the lake for a guy's day. It was a lot of fun. I'm glad I have those memories..." Ethan's voice trailed off as he remembered the talks and the laughter they had shared.

Jonathon smiled, "Ethan, he was so proud of you and Conner. After Conner was born, your dad and I talked about the challenges you would face as a new father. Having a child changes the dynamics of your home and of being a husband. Your dad talked with me about his commitment to walk alongside you and be that partner in faith with you on your journey. I am certain you would be talking with him today if the Lord had not called him home."

Ethan nodded as he let the picture soak in. He imagined how great it would have been to talk with his dad about this struggle.

"I am grateful that you contacted me, Ethan. Since your dad died, I have not yet built the same partnership with another man. Grief and loss take time to process and move through. But when you read the words of Jesus and the epistles in the New Testament, you can see that this is the relationship we are called to have with each other in the church. I would describe it as men walking through life together. Or even better, as men walking with God, together. I say that because God has promised to dwell in us and to walk with us in life. In 2 Corinthians 6, we are called the 'temple of the living God', and '...God said, I will dwell in them and walk among them; and I will be their God, and they shall be My people'" (2 Corinthians 6:16).

"That's an amazing image, Jonathon," Ethan responded. "I'm imagining how it would be, knowing every day that another man has your back and is walking with you through the struggles of life. Then to see that God is there with the two of you is cool! Thank you for telling me how my dad had committed to walking close to me those last two years, and explaining to me why that mattered so much to him. That means a lot to me."

"These relationships are real life-changers, Ethan. This is a big ask for a man with a young family and a very busy life, but what do you think about partnering with me, and us walking with God, through life together? We would commit to spending regular time with each other, praying, studying scripture, and building our lives and our homes on God's truth. God will shape each of our lives, preparing and equipping us to endure the troubles of life. That solid foundation is essential for our work, our family life, our friendships, and our community of fellowship in the church. Our knowledge of God from the Bible equips us to destroy those fortresses of speculation and to take lying thoughts captive to the obedience of Christ."

Ethan's smile reflected the encouragement he felt deep inside. "Yes! Let's do this. Thank you, Jonathon!"

"Great! I'm excited about this! When we meet next week, I think we need to go back in scripture to the very beginning, to Genesis. We need to understand the truth of how God created us, and what that means for our lives today. I'd like to pray now, and ask God to direct our steps as we start down this narrow way, walking together with Him."

Both men leaned in as they bowed their heads and opened their hearts to their Creator. Together, they asked God to work in and through their friendship to teach and transform them to be the men He created them to be.

Discussion and Discipline

- Are there difficult or troubling situations or circumstances in your life that you have been facing alone? Would it help if you could talk about it with someone you trust and respect? Are you willing to be transparent and trust someone to face that struggle with you?

- What fears would you need to face if you considered building this kind of friendship with another man? How can you overcome those fears and step out in faith?

- Only the man who first tells himself the truth is able and willing to share that truth with another man. Are there truths that you have been avoiding in your life? How might it bring you relief to talk through these tough issues with someone you trust?

- In Matthew 28:20, Jesus assures you He is "with you always, even to the end of the age." In 2 Corinthians 6:16, God promises He will dwell in us and will walk among us. That promise is an amazing encouragement as we trudge through long days. How encouraging would it be if you had a strong, committed friendship and partnership with another man who shares your faith and values?

- Though scripture calls for such trusting friendships, people rarely practice them. Why do you think men avoid or are unwilling to engage in such a valuable experience?

FOUNDATIONS OF FAITH

God's Design, Sin's Corruption, and Christ's
Redemption

DDS Publishing

Chapter Two

Created in the Image of God

Designed for Relationship

Ethan and Jonathon enjoyed a hearty breakfast together and caught up on family updates and significant events that had occurred over the past week since they had last met. As they pushed their empty plates aside, Jonathon suggested that each time they meet, they take some time to pray for one another and for their families and their church.

Ethan felt uncomfortable praying together at the table in the restaurant, but that only lasted a few moments. He felt courageous, as he knew God was there with him and Jonathon, together.

When they finished praying, Ethan expressed his anticipation of the day's discussion. "Jonathon, I've been reading in Genesis, trying to get a jump on what we'll be talking about today. I'm curious!"

Jonathon smiled at Ethan's enthusiasm; he was thankful for Ethan's desire to learn and understand what God had to say in His word about his life and faith. "Wonderful! Let's crack open our Bibles and go right to the beginning."

RELATIONSHIP TO OTHERS

Genesis describes how God spoke creation into existence. He formed the structure and order of the earth and its seasons, and He created all animate creatures and inanimate objects. This is when and where we discover and understand the how and why of man's existence, purpose, and meaningful identity.

In the beginning, God created man (the whole of humanity) in His image; according to His likeness, male and female He created them. Here we have an explicit reference to the Trinity, the triune God who is the Father, Son, and Holy Spirit:

Then God said, "Let Us make man in Our image, according to Our likeness; and let them rule over the fish of the sea and over the birds of the sky and over the cattle and over all the earth, and over every creeping thing that creeps on the earth." God created man in His own image, in the image of God He created him; male and female He created them. (Genesis 1:26-27)

The "Us/Our" nature of God's image ("Let *Us* make man in *Our* image") is particular and important; an "I/me" outcome for man is not an accurate or complete image (reflection) of an "Us/Our" model. God is not individual, but is complex and three-in-one. This is a profound mystery. That is the complex image which mankind reflects. This first statement, "Let Us make man in Our image... male and female He created them," demonstrates intention and specificity about the design of man. It informs us of important characteristics of man's design which contribute to a life that is orderly, meaningful, and purposeful. And when those characteristics of man's design are out of alignment, turmoil and chaos are the outcome in a man's life.

The Triune God created and designed the whole of mankind to reflect His image. An individual person is an incomplete reflection of that image. God designed mankind to function and be in relationships with others, and those in relationships with others are greater than the sum of their individual persons. When essential engagement in relationships with others is unavailable for a prolonged period, a man struggles and suffers. An individual who is isolated from relationships is not missing parts, like an automobile that is missing tires, but is more like a cake which was baked without the egg or milk. It may still look like a cake should (and it *is* a cake), but the flavor or texture will be off. In this same way, the flavor and texture of the life of an individual suffers when disconnected from caring relationships with others. But when all the proper ingredients of the recipe are mixed in, the cake looks and tastes great. In the same way, when we are engaged in healthy relationships with many others, our life is rich and more interesting.

Each person has a long list of relationships with others. There's your spouse, your parents, your friends, coworkers, neighbors, the guy that rides on the same train each day with you, the checkout girl at the grocery store, the neighbor boy who mows your lawn, and dozens of others! Some relationships comprise just a moment or two each day, or each week, but they are a part of who we are. We interact differently with one person than we do with another. Maybe we feel safer and can open up our soul with someone more than others, or maybe they share the same strong interest in football, or fast cars, as us.

The relationship we have with others provides a canvas upon which our expression of self is on display and experienced. We discover, or unveil, a more complete picture of ourselves when we live in relationship with others. That picture may encourage or disappoint us, but it is real. The process of talking out loud with someone about new ideas, or discussing potential solutions to a problem, is helpful in developing new concepts.

Relationships bring flavor and texture to our thoughts as we put them into words and share them out loud with others. Author C. S. Lewis describes this regarding friendships in his book, "The Four Loves". Lewis enjoyed a close mutual friendship with J. R. R. Tolkien and Charles Williams. He describes how his relationship with Ronald (J. R. R. Tolkien) changed after the death of Charles:

> In each of my friends there is something that only some other friend can fully bring out. By myself I am not large enough to call the whole man into activity; I want other lights than my own to show all his facets. Now that Charles is dead, I shall never again see Ronald's reaction to a specifically Charles joke. Far from having more of Ronald, having him 'to myself' now that Charles is away, I have less of Ronald... In this, Friendship exhibits a glorious "nearness by resemblance" to heaven itself where the very multitude of the blessed (which no man can number) increases the fruition which each of us has of God. For every soul, seeing Him in her own way, doubtless communicates that unique vision to all the rest. (Lewis, C. S. (1971). *The Four Loves*. Mariner Books)

This is the complexity and mystery of being made in the image of God and explains why we need and desire meaningful and healthy relationships with others. This is also why we often act dysfunctionally when we are isolated from others. When we understand how our Creator designed us, it brings clarity to the value of relationships in our lives. It helps to make sense of our struggles and joys in those relationships and guides us in setting relational expectations.

RELATIONSHIP WITH GOD

The most important relationship for a man is his relationship with God. God is the Creator, and man is His creation; man functioning in alignment with the design of this relationship is key to the peaceful harmony and sanctity of life in the Garden. The nature of man's relationship with God is best described as having a posture of humility. Humility lives within the creature who knows they exist and have life because of the will and generosity of the Creator. Andrew Murray describes it this way:

> Humility, the place of entire dependence on God, is, from the very nature of things, the first duty and the highest virtue of the creature... (Murray, A. (2001). *Humility*. Bethany House Publishers)

Adam, having been just formed from the dust by God's hands, knows that he exists, and that he exists by God's grace and desire. God had breathed His own breath into Adam's lungs and given him life. That life was not just a once only disbursement, but God energized every breath, every heartbeat, and every movement by His eternal power. Every moment of Adam's life was an act of God alone. The recognition and acknowledgment that God is everything, and that man is an empty vessel into which God breathes life each moment, is humility. Humility defines the proper posture of man toward his God. Humility is at the core of the creation's worship of God. Worship means to bow down low in reverence and adoration. In the garden of Eden, this perfect place of creation, Adam and Eve loved and worshipped (or adored) their Creator!

WE–NOT JUST ME

Ethan felt like his eyes were being opened to a new aspect of life he had never seen before, even though it had always been right in front of him. "This explains why being connected with you to talk about the stuff that's going on in my life matters so much!" he said. "It's almost like I've been blind to a huge part of what life is about. I can't imagine what my life would be like without Alicia and Connor. It also helps to make sense of why my dad's death was so hard to deal with!"

He sat back and carefully framed his next statement and question, "Jonathon, I always understood the Bible to say that 'I', as an individual, am made in the image of God, separate from connection with anyone else. But if it is saying that God made *us* in the image of God, then it seems to follow that being in relationship and even *how* I am in a relationship with those around me, takes on a much greater importance. That makes sense when I think about you and I walking through life together on the narrow way, caring for our families, and connecting with others in the church. But does it matter whether those I connect with are Christian or non-Christian? How should I think about non-Christians and being in a relationship with them?"

Jonathon smiled and asked, "Is this a work-related question? Are you wondering if there is any value in working together, cooperating, and collaborating with those who don't share your faith? Let's look at Romans, chapter 12. The Bible talks here about our relationships with other Christians, 'We, who are many, are one body in Christ,' and also about relating to non-Christians: 'Bless those who persecute you... Respect what is right in the sight of all men. If possible, so far as it depends on you, be at peace with *all* men' (Romans 12:4-18).

"Ethan, remember that sin affects and taints our relationships with everyone, whether or not they are Christians. God gave His Son because He loves the world, not just those who respond in faith. In 2 Peter 3:9, the Bible says that God 'is patient... not wishing for any to perish but for all to come to repentance.' Love should be the motivation behind our engagement with all people, non-Christian or Christian."

Ethan pondered this for a few moments, staring at the coffee cup on the table in front of him. He confessed, "I know I have had very little care for, or even interest in, my coworkers, and I sure don't love them. My thinking and my heart would need to change toward them in a big way! I'm not even sure that I can do that. Honestly, I just can't see how that could happen; God would have to do a miracle in my heart. Jonathon, will you pray with me about my attitude?"

"Yes, let's do that now." Jonathon and Ethan bowed their heads and prayed together that God would give Ethan a heart of compassion and care for his coworkers, and that he would learn the discipline of reflecting the love and compassion of Christ in his workplace.

Discussion and Discipline

- How does it affect your view toward others when you consider that reflecting the image of God depends on you being in a relationship with them? When you see that someone thinks differently about things than you do, do you find that to be valuable or annoying? Why?

- Romans 12 gives us guidelines on relating with other Christians and with non-Christians. Has it been important for you to steward your relationships with both in a way that honors God and is true to His word? What steps might you consider taking to do that more completely?

- Are you challenged to love the world as God does (John 3:16), knowing that God is waiting and wishing for all to come to repentance (2 Peter 3:9)? Is there any person you have a difficult time tolerating, much less loving? What small steps can you take in that direction to better steward your relationship with them?

- Think of what C.S. Lewis experienced concerning his friend, Ronald. There were facets of Ronald's personality that were no longer evident after their friend, Charles, died. Have you observed that unique elements of someone's personality are more or less prevalent, depending on who is present? Do you act or respond differently, depending on the individuals or group with which you are associating at the time?

- The first and most important relationship we have is with God. Andrew Murray writes that "Humility, the place of entire dependence on God, is, from the very nature of things, the first duty and the highest virtue of the creature." (Murray, A. (2001). *Humility*. Bethany House Publishers). Does humility, that place of entire dependence on God, describe your relationship with Him? How so, or why not?

Chapter Three

Created for Stewardship

God Gives His Creation Work to Do

When they met next, Jonathon asked Ethan to share with him how he was doing with building relationships at the office.

"I'm surprised, Jonathon, but I think it's going well! I am seeing people in a new light. It's not perfect, of course. Some people are going to be harder than others for me to connect with. But there's no doubt that I'm becoming more aware of my coworkers, and even noticing when they're having good days and bad days. I've even encouraged and given support to a couple of them who are experiencing personal problems and struggles."

"That's great, Ethan! It sounds like you are leaning into the understanding that those relationships are meaningful, whether or not they are Christians."

"God is in the life-changing business!" Ethan gave a sheepish look. "Even as we prayed that God would change my heart toward my coworkers, I had low expectations of ever feeling different. But even in this short amount of time, I have noticed that valuing those around me gives my whole day more significance." Ethan paused, then continued, "Though I'm still feeling flat about my job overall. I can't help but wonder if I'm just in the wrong job, and if maybe that's why I'm lacking motivation at work."

Jonathon pressed Ethan for more details. "What type of work are you hoping to do instead? What work would fit your gifts and talents better?"

"Oh, it's not that," Ethan said. "Marketing is what I've always been interested in, and I'm good at it. It's just that after so many years with one company, there's no new excitement or intrigue. I guess I am just wondering what something new would be like. Work has been such a drudgery, but maybe that's because having to work is part of the consequences of sin in this fallen world."

"Hold on there!" Jonathon replied. "I don't know that I agree that work resulted from man's sin. We should check that out in scripture. One of the first things God did following creation was to give man a job to do. Let's go back to Genesis and look closer at what was going on before the serpent and sin knocked everything out of whack."

STEWARDING THE GARDEN

After creating man, God planted the garden of Eden and placed the man there to "cultivate it and keep it" (Genesis 2:8, 15). With very little fanfare, the Bible describes how God assigned man to care for the garden which He had planted. God instructed man that, along with his duty to cultivate and care for the garden, he may eat from any tree of the garden, "but from the tree of the knowledge of good and evil you shall not eat" (Genesis 2:16-17). This assignment, to care for someone else's property, is called a stewardship. A master entrusts a steward with the care and well-being of the property, belongings, or resources of another, as if it were their own.

From the beginning, God prescribed that man should be engaged and entrusted with purposeful, productive work or activity in relationship to others. In today's economic terms, we might refer to such a person as a business owner, or as an employee of a business. God entrusts the business owner with a trade, product, or service to provide to others. The business owner entrusts the employee with the responsibility to assemble, care for, sell, promote, or provide the wares or services of the business.

Jesus had a great deal to say about stewardship in the gospels. He speaks of "the faithful and sensible steward, whom his master will put in charge of his servants" (Luke 12:42-43). It is clear that faithfulness in smaller things is the criteria for determining when a steward might be eligible for promotion or advancement to greater responsibilities (Luke 16:10-12).

God places great value on dependable and consistent work in service to others. In 1 Thessalonians 4:11-12, the apostle urges those in the church, "To make it your ambition to lead a quiet life and attend to your own business and work with your hands, just as we commanded you, so that you will behave properly toward outsiders and not be in any need."

In the second letter to the church of Thessalonica, he reviews the stewardship and responsibility of work with the church.

For even when we were with you, we used to give you this order: if anyone is not willing to work, then he is not to eat either. For we hear that some among you are leading an undisciplined life, doing no work at all, but acting like busybodies. Now such persons we command and exhort in the Lord Jesus Christ to work in quiet fashion and eat their own bread (2 Thessalonians 3:10-12).

1 Timothy 5:8 speaks about those who are irresponsible in caring for their families: "If anyone does not provide for those of his household, he has denied the faith and is worse than an unbeliever."

In the letter written to the church in Philippi, Paul instructed them to:

Do nothing from selfishness or empty conceit, but with humility of mind regard one another as more important than yourselves; do not merely look out for your own personal interests, but also for the interests of others (Philippians 2:3-4).

This admonition says to regard "one another," or all those with whom you have a relationship, as more important than yourself. A man's family is the most important group of "one anothers" in his life. His self-interest suggests he should have excitement or gain personal enjoyment from his work. But God's word instructs him to place his highest value on the care and provision for his family. If an employment change is to be considered, it should be a thoughtful process which prepares his family for what to expect, and which does not place them in unnecessary financial jeopardy.

WORK: RESPONSIBILITY OR PLEASURE?

"Ethan, how are you now understanding what the Bible teaches us about work, stewardship, and employment?" Jonathon asked. "I wonder if you have been expecting your work to be a source of pleasure for you?"

"Wow!" exclaimed Ethan. "This challenges my view of my job. I'm not sure what shaped my perspective, but I've always thought that a person's job should be a 'perfect' fit for them… whatever that means! I guess I felt like my job should be enjoyable each day I was working; so yeah, I think you could say I expected my work to always bring me pleasure. So, when work hasn't felt pleasurable, it seems like something is wrong and I've thought I needed to fix it.

"I had never understood 'cultivating and caring' for the garden as a responsibility, or a job, that God had given to Adam – that Adam was the steward of God's garden. And this was all before sin even entered the picture. I suppose Adam may have even sweated a bit when he was working to cultivate the garden. It sounds weird to even say that, because I never would have thought that Adam was 'working' before sin entered the picture!"

Jonathon nodded in agreement. "You know, Ethan, it's very rational to think that every breath we take into our lungs and every hour of the day that our hearts beat are resources of life and time that God has entrusted to our care. We are stewards of those hours, one hour at a time. In the same way, we are stewards of the relationships we have with those around us, and we are to be mindful of our responsibilities and care for them."

Ethan winced as he realized, "The 1 Timothy 5:8 reference puts Alicia's concerns into perspective for me. She has been a little freaked out about my frustration with my job. I think I need to elevate the value I place on providing for my family, and for ensuring my wife's peace of mind."

"You've nailed it, Ethan," Jonathan encouraged him. "Your disciplined and consistent work as a provider for your family shows faithfulness to God as His steward. It also shows genuine love and care for your wife and son. That is faithful stewardship!"

"Scripture seems pretty straightforward about work, doesn't it? If I'm honest about it, Alicia has been trying to tell me this for weeks now." Ethan ran his finger around the rim of his coffee cup and stared into the dark liquid as he asked, "Jonathon, here is what bothers me the most. I think I've become self-centered about my job and how it makes me feel. I don't even appreciate having this job! How did I get to be so selfish, and then to be clueless about how that affects my wife?"

"Hmmm... that's a good question, Ethan." Jonathon flipped to the next page in Genesis and pointed at the page, saying, "I think the answer to your question is in chapter three. Let's dig into that next time we meet. But now, let's pray God will open our eyes to see how we can be better stewards of the life and responsibilities that He has entrusted to us."

The two men bowed their heads and together lifted their prayers to God. They asked Him to give them eyes to see the stewardship that was entrusted to them in their homes, their employment, and their church. They also asked God for willing hearts to be faithful stewards, to carry out the responsibilities of each day.

Discussion and Discipline

- From the beginning, God designed man to work as a steward of what God would entrust to man. What employment, business, or volunteer work has God entrusted to your care?

- In 2 Thessalonians 3:10-12, we read, "if anyone is not willing to work, then he is not to eat either." How would you respond to someone who said they felt this statement lacked love or compassion? Is there an age limit to that statement, or circumstances which would be outside the parameters of that statement?

- Read 1 Timothy 5:8. What does this tell you about the value God places on your responsibility to provide for your family? Is this scripture too harsh? Why or why not?

- Read the parable of the talents in Matthew 25:14-30. Discuss the principles and application of what Jesus is teaching here. What is He saying about taking risks, a person's motivation, playing it "safe", fear of failure, and the "worthless" slave's view of his master? What does this parable teach us regarding our work or employment?

- 1 Peter 4:10 says, "As each one has received a special gift, employ it in serving one another as good stewards of the manifold grace of God." God gives us the stewardship and instructs us to employ our gifts in service to one another. He then says in verse 11 that we are to do this "so that in all things God may be glorified through Jesus Christ." Have you considered that your work, or the employment of your gifts, results in God being glorified? Think of an example.

- In Luke 12:42 and 16:10, Jesus describes stewards as being faithful and sensible. He said that being faithful in a minor thing shows a steward will also be faithful in much. What are the signs or indicators of being faithful? Are you exhibiting those indicators?

- You may think that your impact and influence should be large, loud, and impressive. How does that align with the admonition we read in 1 Thessalonians 4:11-12, and 2 Thessalonians 3:11-12, to "lead a quiet life and attend to your own business and work with your hands", to "behave properly toward outsiders", and to "work in a quiet fashion and eat [your] own bread"?

Chapter Four

Trouble and Treason

The Rise of Self, and the Fall of Man

Ethan arrived at the restaurant early for his next meeting with Jonathon. Since they last met, he had continued to be troubled by the unappreciative attitude he had developed toward his work, and how clueless he was about the resulting impact on Alicia. He wondered if he should sit down with her and talk about what he was seeing about these things and tell her it was hard for him to admit that he was seeing himself as self-centered. He could see how self-absorbed he was in his own feelings and desires, and was understanding how his discontentment at work was affecting her. But he couldn't bring himself to have that conversation with her; it was almost terrifying to even consider it. He thought he was a better husband than that. In some ways, it was like the more he understood, the worse he discovered things were! He hoped gaining more insight through time with Jonathon and learning from scripture would help bring some resolution to all he was wrestling with.

When Jonathon arrived, he expressed surprise to see Ethan had already settled in at the booth where they would share breakfast. "You must have woken up early this morning!" he grinned.

"Yeah, you could say that," Ethan responded. "I'm eager to talk about what's next in Genesis. You said chapter 3 might hold the answers to why I've been selfish and not very thoughtful toward my wife."

"I see," Jonathon nodded. "Let's get right to it, then. This is important."

They both opened their Bibles to Genesis 3 to read the familiar story of Eve's temptation...

HAS GOD SAID...?

In chapter three of Genesis, we watch as trouble enters man's life for the first time since he began his stewardship of the garden. The serpent tempted the woman to disobey God through the pride of her own reasoning. Pride is the wickedness which had caused Lucifer's fall from heaven. Now the serpent was intent upon injecting the same poisonous evil into man's ears and mind. Through his sly and deceptive dialog that questioned God's explicit instruction, he tempted the woman to think for herself (or, *her Self*), instead of trusting in God.

Man had no natural defense against this spiritual poison, and the infection was clear the moment Eve fell into the trap of choosing to measure God's words against the serpent's words. In his book, The Kingdom of God is Within You, Andrew Murray captures the crisis with these words:

> The temptation with which Satan came to man in Paradise really meant this — would he [man] with his whole heart yield to God as Father and Master, giving him His place and doing His will alone? Or would he not do his own will, and let Self-rule as master in his own house? Alas! that fatal choice. God was dethroned and cast out of His temple, and Self set upon the throne. (Murray, A. (2015). *The Kingdom of God is Within You*. Ichthus Publications).

As discussing with the serpent progressed, the poisonous seed of pride was implanted in Eve's heart. It germinated and grew until the newly formed Self sat down on the throne to rule over her being. She measured God's limiting and restrictive commands against the enticing and more favorable pronouncements of the serpent. She elevated her own assessment of the tree and its fruit above what God had said (Genesis 3:1-13). The seed of pride is that which feeds Self and fuels its demand for autonomy. It grows into every kind of sin and evil, and so it is the mainstay of Satan's arsenal in his assault upon man. Satan is determined to destroy man's posture of humility (that place of entire dependence on God) toward his Creator.

For Eve, or for us to suggest God's word is inconclusive on any matter, is the height of arrogance and self-importance. The woman decided to consider that "the tree was good for food, and that it was a delight to the eyes, and that the tree was desirable to make one wise" (Genesis 3:6). Here we see that the woman is reasoning between God's view and Self-view, weighing both views as if they were equal in credibility, thus elevating and equating Self with God.

After pride convinced Eve to consider this additional information, she chose Self over God. She first decided her Self-view on the issue was better informed and more desirable than God's instruction. Then she decided to ignore the prohibition God had set regarding the fruit of the tree. This is that which separated her from God, that moment when pride elevated Self to equal, and then higher standing than God. She ate the fruit, then gave it to her husband, and he ate.

Eating the fruit was the sin of disobedience, but Self-elevation by pride gave birth to that sin and brought trouble and death to all of mankind. The development and awakening of Self within the heart of man was the serpent's deceptive scheme to poison all of future mankind with pride and Self-rule. This was how he would separate mankind from his God. Now each man must face the daily testing of pride and "Self-rule", which stirs up the same compulsions with which Eve struggled. James catalogs this struggle for man, saying:

> Let no one say when he is tempted, "I am being tempted by God"; for God cannot be tempted by evil, and He Himself does not tempt anyone. But each one is tempted when he is carried away and enticed by his own lust. Then when lust has conceived, it gives birth to sin; and when sin is accomplished, it brings forth death. Do not be deceived, my beloved brethren. (James 1:13–16)

Now, because of man's fall from his humble relationship with God, Self remains enthroned in the heart of men, to rule the lives of men and to cause division and chaos in all relationships.

COVERED AND DRIVEN OUT OF THE GARDEN

After sin had corrupted mankind (the rise of Self, and the "fall" of man), God visited the garden. The man and his wife heard God walking in the garden and "hid themselves from the presence of the Lord God among the trees of the garden" (Genesis 3:8).

Though they know God is omnipotent, they are like a small child playing hide and seek, who covers their eyes and thinks they are invisible!

God calls out to the man, "Where are you?" (Genesis 3:9). The man's answer is evidence of having eaten the forbidden fruit. He answers and explains that when he heard God in the garden, he experienced fear and shame at being naked for the first time, so he hid himself. God asks, "Who told you that you were naked? Have you eaten from the tree of which I commanded you not to eat?" (Genesis 3:11). God's question, asking, "Who told you?", is a tacit reference to the new character in the story of man—Self.

The admission by the man that he now was afraid and ashamed is revealing. After his sin, he was Self-conscious, Self-aware, and Self-condemning. It is the case that each time we succumb to the elevation of Self over God's authority, fear and shame flood our being. This results in great distress, which is difficult to face, and that is why we "hide" in many activities and behavior. God calls to us, "Where are you?" We choose whether to turn a deaf ear to His voice or to confess that we are ashamed and naked.

After choosing Self-rule, the man and his wife each attempt to protect the new ruler (Self) enthroned in their hearts by pointing the finger of blame at others for their actions. God pronounces the devastating consequences for their pride and sin on all of mankind and nature. After God declares His judgment, He addresses Adam and Eve's greatest immediate need by making the first sacrificial covering for their naked and sinful condition: "The Lord God made garments of skin for Adam and his wife, and clothed them" (Genesis 3:21).

To close out this sad chapter of deception, treason, and "Self-protection," God drove man out of the garden of Eden. Man could no longer dwell and walk with God in this special place. Now enslaved in the state of "Self-rule", He knew that man might "take also from the tree of life, and eat, and live forever," and remain in this terrible state for eternity (Genesis 3:22-24). Mercifully, God drove man out of the garden and stationed a guard with a flaming sword "which turned every direction" to keep man from accessing the tree of life.

ETHAN... WHERE ARE YOU?

"I can picture Adam and Eve hiding in the bushes because of their shame, when God came walking through the garden, and that's a lot like what I'm dealing with right now," Ethan confessed. "Self-protection has been high on my priority list, and I understand now how that came to be through Adam and Eve. My selfishness has affected Alicia, and I am naked and ashamed, like Adam. I'm the one who is hiding from God and my wife."

Jonathon spoke comforting words to Ethan. "Ethan, just as God sacrificed and shed the blood of animals to make coverings for Adam and Eve there in the garden, you know Jesus shed His blood on the cross and covers you with His robe of righteousness. His sacrifice for your sin is complete when you first profess your faith in Him, and also as you confess sin while you walk on the narrow way as His disciple (Isaiah 61:10). You know Jesus has redeemed you by His shed blood on Calvary. You've known that to be true since you were a child.

"Acknowledging our Self, pride, and sin can be challenging and agonizing, making us fear judgment and try to conceal ourselves. That's why humility is such an essential characteristic in the life of the Christian man. In humility, we recognize our dependence upon God and His grace for everything, and the exposure of pride and Self propels us to greater dependence on God. Humility is the evidence of reconciliation through Christ to the natural creature/Creator relationship."

"I have a question about pride," Ethan pondered out loud. "I guess I have always thought there was a distinction between arrogance, which is obviously sinful, and pride. Arrogance is being puffed up and thinking more highly of yourself than you should. But isn't it good to have pride in doing a good job, or in being a good husband?"

"Let's think about that for a moment," Jonathon replied. "Tell me, what would be the basis on which you might conclude that you are a 'good' husband? How do you measure that?"

Ethan mulled over this simple question. Several times he began to answer, but then stopped short as he wrestled with Jonathon's question. Finally, he sighed and said, "Well, I'm faithful to my wife. I help her out around the house pretty often, and I make sure we go to church. There are lots of other good things I do too! All those things seem to make sense, but my answers sound like I am defending myself. Maybe I think I'm a good husband because I want to *believe* I'm a good husband.

"I suppose I would need to know how Alicia measures being a good husband, and how God measures it. Both would be important. In fact, before we started meeting together and learning from scripture, I know I would have said that I was proud of being a good husband. Yet, now I realize that my Self-centered view on my job has been causing a lot of anxiety for my wife, and I feel like I've been anything but a good husband."

"Ethan, a minute ago I asked you how you measure being a good husband," Jonathon said. "But a better question may be, '*why* are you measuring that?' You see, Self likes to measure things to prove its superiority and to elevate and puff up. Humility is simple. It is living in obedience to God and in service to those around you. You don't need to be 'proud' of being a good husband. You just need to *be* one because you love God, and you love your wife. The Bible teaches us the measure of a good husband in Ephesians, chapter five. It says, 'Husbands, love your wives, just as Christ also loved the church and gave Himself up for her...' (Ephesians 5:25), and '...husbands ought also to love their own wives as their own bodies. He who loves his own wife loves himself; for no one ever hated his own flesh, but nourishes and cherishes it, just as Christ also does the church, because we are members of His body' (Ephesians 5:28-30). Ethan, our purpose as husbands is to love our wife just as Christ also loved the church. Christ gave His life for the sake of the church. You see, being a good husband is only possible as you walk in humility with God and with your wife.

"We should talk more about this over the next few weeks. But now I need to get home to mow the yard, and then I'm going to take my lovely wife for a drive in the country. Marie loves it when the two of us go driving! And it would be good for you to spend some time with Alicia and open up to her, hiding nothing. Don't let pride and Self stop you from loving your wife in this way. Talk with her about what we are learning about Self, pride, and sin, and ask her what she needs and desires from you, as a husband."

Ethan smiled. "Yes, that will be the next important conversation I have today. Thank you, Jonathon. I needed this more than I even realized. Something tells me that the next few months of us meeting together may be life-changing for me!"

"It will be life-changing for both of us!" exclaimed Jonathon. "Ethan, let's pray together before we head out."

They bowed their heads there at the table, and Jonathon prayed for Ethan and Alicia, Conner, and for Ethan's coworkers. He thanked God for meeting there with the two of them and teaching them together, and he thanked God for walking with them as they continued on this journey of faith. Ethan thanked God for the impact Jonathon's friendship was having on his life and prayed for both Jonathon and Marie. He confessed his sinful and selfish attitudes and praised God for forgiveness and salvation through Christ's sacrifice on the cross.

Discussion and Discipline

- Have you noticed how, just as the serpent asked Eve, "Has God said…?", Christians are likewise tempted to question God's word? What personal examples can you think of? How have you handled that test? What can you do differently that will be more effective in honoring God and walking in humility with Him?

- In which areas of your life do you feel Self-sufficient, where you have things under control? Is it true that you have things under control, or is there some Self-deception going on? With humility being defined as entire dependence on God, what areas of your life do you view with humility?

- Andrew Murray defines pride as "the loss of humility" (Murray, A. (2001). *Humility*. Bethany House Publishers). With that definition in mind, it would follow that in the areas of life where one feels they "have things under control" and that they are not dependent on God, pride is the underlying factor. Is that difficult for you to consider? If so, why? What will be the cost for you to face the truth of how dependent you are on God?

- After Self became enthroned through pride in the hearts of Adam and Eve, they hid in the bushes when they heard God walking in the garden. Adam explained to God that he was afraid because he was naked; so he hid. In what ways do we "hide" from God, or others, to protect our vulnerabilities? Is there a particular area of your life in which you are hiding from God?

- Ethan recognizes that Self and pride cause trouble for him, his marriage, and his work. Can you identify situations in your life where Self and pride cause or contribute to problems and trouble?

Chapter Five

Denying Self

Taking up Your Cross Daily

Ethan couldn't wait to share with Jonathon at their next breakfast together how his view of work was changing. "It's an amazing difference already," he said. "The biggest change is in how I am connecting with some of my coworkers now. I know I'm just beginning to be intentional about this, but it is like I am seeing some of them for the first time, and I'm getting to know each of them as a person. I was so disconnected before!"

"That's great!" exclaimed Jonathon. He appreciated how Ethan had taken things to heart from their last discussion and then acted on it. "How do you feel about your follow-up conversation with Alicia?"

Ethan's eyes glistened as he described the very difficult, but wonderful, conversation he had with his wife. "Leesh was shocked at first that I was admitting I realized how selfish I had been acting. But as I shared about seeing from scripture that it was my responsibility to be a steward of this job to provide and care for our family, she gave me the biggest hug. She was crying tears of joy in my arms. I feel we are closer to each other now than we have been in a long time!"

"That's beautiful, Ethan. I'm so thankful for what God is doing in your life and home!" Jonathon shared he had also found after their conversation that he had a renewed awareness of stewarding each hour given by God, and his relationships with family and neighbors. He opened his Bible and said, "The last time we wrapped our heads around how trouble started in the garden of Eden with the poison of pride and man's rebellion by choosing Self-rule. We should look at how that needs to be addressed for us as Christian men, and what scripture says about Self and following Christ. Let's look at Luke 9..."

DEALING WITH SELF

Jesus is very direct in telling His disciples about the animosity of pride and self with being His follower. He addresses this in Luke 9:23, "And He was saying to them all, 'If anyone wishes to come after Me, he must deny himself, and take up his cross daily and follow Me.'"

This is the opposite of the choice that was made in the garden, which was a choice for pride and Self-rule. The choice for Self-rule was an act of rebellion and treason against God, and put man at enmity with God. That means that man became God's enemy. Reconciliation of man with God cannot be possible with man's retention of treasonous Self-rule. Therefore, Jesus declares that if anyone wishes to come after Him, the first step is to deny Self, to dethrone, and renounce Self-rule.

But that is not a "one and done" act. The denial of Self continues with taking up your cross daily. Jesus saying we must take up our cross daily should cause us to snap to attention! This is an easy sentence to read and move past, but it is a crucial factor for living each new day in faith through Christ. As Christians in the West, our view of the cross is as a cherished symbol or icon. The cross communicates the substitutionary death of Christ in atonement for our sins and symbolizes access through Christ to God's grace, forgiveness, and love. While true, limiting our understanding of the cross to this symbolism is not helpful for understanding Jesus' words here in Luke. The cross had one purpose: it was an instrument of torturous suffering, and its use always ended with an excruciating death. The convicted criminal, condemned to death, carried the cross upon his own shoulders, suffering terribly as he was driven by whips to the place of death by crucifixion.

Self, given its life through pride, is that entity which must bear the cross to the place of its death. Self-denial is the most counter-cultural act you will ever observe, or in which you will ever take part. It includes crucifying the flesh with its passions and desires (Galatians 5:24), saying "no" to ungodliness and living a disciplined, godly life (Titus 2:11-13). Denial of Self values the interests of others and not just your own (Philippians 2:4-8), seeks what is best for others instead of what is best for yourself (1 Corinthians 10:24), and surrenders the pursuit of status, power, and prominence over others. (Luke 14:7-11).

This is a hard path to walk through life, and it is very costly. In Luke 14:27-33, Jesus again says everyone who wants to be His disciple must carry his own cross, and He advises the listener to "calculate the cost" before deciding to follow Him. He gives the example of deciding to build a tower, and, after laying the foundation, discovering there are not enough funds to finish the project. The second example Jesus gives is of a king who considers going out to battle against another king. He needs to evaluate if his army is strong enough to win the battle. If his army is not strong enough, he will instead need to negotiate a peace agreement. So it is that Jesus says we must count the cost of following Him. What is that cost? It costs *everything!* Jesus makes this statement in Luke 14:33, that might sound harsh and unreasonable to the reader: "So then, none of you can be My disciple who does not give up all his own possessions."

Why would Jesus set such a severe standard for discipleship? This was not the only time Jesus touched on a nerve regarding possessions. In Matthew 19, a wealthy young man asked Jesus, "What good thing shall I do that I may obtain eternal life?" Jesus tells him he must keep the commandments, and the man says he has kept them. But he knows he is still lacking something! Jesus gets right to the heart of the matter by saying to him, "If you wish to be complete, go and sell your possessions and give to the poor, and you will have treasure in heaven; and come, follow Me" (Matthew 19:16-26).

The young man is heartbroken and goes away grieving, because he owned much property. A shallow reading of this statement may leave the impression that Jesus wants His followers to own nothing and live a life of poverty and destitution. But that conclusion would miss the point.

The problem for the wealthy young man was Self-rule. He proved this when he proudly told Jesus of his good Self-performance in keeping the commandments. But yet he knew he was still lacking what was necessary to gain heaven. Achievement, wealth, performance, accumulation, power, and status are all Self-driven pursuits. They are pitiful efforts to atone for the treasonous sinner and reconcile him to God.

So, Jesus plunged right into the heart of the prideful Self-rule beast by declaring the young man must give away all his wealth, that he must *empty himself and become dependent upon Jesus* in following Him. A return to the posture of humility is pivotal for the decision to deny Self and take up your cross daily to follow Jesus. Jesus is the *only way*, the narrow way to the Father, and He requires the return of the creature to humility, the denial of Self. This place of *entire dependence on God* is essential to restoring the right and natural relationship between the creature and the Creator.

Self does not die quickly, and it does not fade quietly into the shadows. The narrow way is described as a way of suffering. Paul told of his path of suffering the loss of all things, in view of the surpassing value of knowing Christ Jesus:

> But whatever things were gain to me, those things I have counted as loss for the sake of Christ. More than that, I count all things to be loss in view of the surpassing value of knowing Christ Jesus my Lord, for whom I have suffered the loss of all things, and count them but rubbish so that I may gain Christ, and may be found in Him, not having a righteousness of my own derived from the Law, but that which is through faith in Christ, the righteousness which comes from God on the basis of faith, that I may know Him and the power of His resurrection and the fellowship of His sufferings, being conformed to His death; in order that I may attain to the resurrection from the dead. (Philippians 3:7-11)

A life of self-denial also goes hand-in-hand with the willingness to suffer various trials which test the genuineness of our faith (1 Peter 1:6-7), and persecutions because we live a godly life (2 Timothy 3:10-12).

Yes, count the cost of following Jesus! But you must also count the cost of not following Him. We began this study of denying Self with Jesus' words in Luke 9:23. We must return there and continue reading.

> "For whoever wishes to save his life will lose it, but whoever loses his life for My sake, he is the one who will save it. For what is a man profited if he gains the whole world, and loses or forfeits himself?" (Luke 9:24-25)

The cost of "saving" our lives, of grasping onto Self-rule and the trappings of Self-achievement, possessions, and status, is losing our lives for eternity. By holding onto Self, we remain unreconciled to right relationship with our Creator. That is the steepest cost!

A SOBERING CONSIDERATION

This was a serious conversation for Ethan and Jonathon; both felt the weight of the challenge to "count the cost" of their faith, of following Jesus as Christian men, and counting what would be the eternal cost of choosing not to follow Jesus.

"Well, abandoning my faith in Christ is *not* an option!" Ethan said. "But I have to say that I've never viewed my faith in this light before. Adam and Eve's decision to disobey God, and to let pride and Self reign in their lives, resulted in Self causing trouble for all of mankind. I guess I have always thought of Self as a 'problem' and that it would be best if I made some effort to deal with it, *sometime*. But Jesus is drawing a line in the sand on Self, and I need to decide if I'm going to be on the Self side of that line, or on Jesus' side!"

"That's well said, Ethan," Jonathon affirmed. "There can be only one king reigning in our lives, and in Jesus is the only place I have found hope and words of life. My decision stands firm as well! I want us to spend some solid time in prayer this morning, thanking God for His faithful and patient love for us, asking Him to teach us and to walk closely with us as we learn together."

The men found that morning's time of prayer together to be rich and significant. Their mutual commitment to deny Self and follow Jesus at any cost strengthened their bond of fellowship.

Discussion and Discipline

- Jesus said, "If anyone wishes to come after Me, he must deny himself, and take up his cross daily and follow Me." Have you made a conscious decision to deny Self? Has denial of Self been challenging for you?

- Whether you choose to forfeit your soul because you wish to save your life, or you lose your life for Christ's sake and find it, there is an actual cost to your decision. What decision have you made about denying Self and taking up your cross?

- What are the difficult things that you may still need to consider saying "no" to as a follower of Jesus? Are you willing to let go of those things?

- The apostle writes in 1 Peter 1:6-7 that "various trials" demonstrate the proof of your faith by being tested by fire. What trials have you experienced that tested your faith?

- How about taking up your cross daily? What does that look like in your life? Give some examples. What has been the most difficult aspect of denying Self for you?

- What are the things you would have to consider as you count the cost of taking up your cross daily and walking with God? Are you willing to give up everything to follow Jesus?

Chapter Six

Walking Humbly with God

The Place of Entire Dependence on God

"Jonathon," Ethan opened up, "ever since we met last, I've been thinking about our time of prayer, and how you prayed for us. You thanked God for meeting with us and teaching us, and you prayed God would walk closely with us as we walked together on this journey of faith. That picture in my head has become so important, and helps me each day. It means the world to me that you will walk alongside me and help me learn and challenge me to grow in my faith! And picturing that God is also walking with the two of us each day is an amazing thing. To know that He is always there makes being a steward of every hour very real!"

"Yes, I know what you mean, Ethan." Jonathon opened his Bible to the book of Micah. "In fact, that's what I wanted us to look at first in our time together today. Ethan, let's read from Micah 6:8."

WHAT DOES THE LORD REQUIRE OF ME?

> He has told you, O man, what is good; and what does the Lord require of you but to do justice, to love kindness, and to walk humbly with your God? (Micah 6:8)

There are three broad areas of conduct identified here in Micah, and each of them pertains to a man's relationship with others. First, to do justice means a man is not to cheat others, and he ensures others receive fair treatment. Second, to love kindness describes a gentle and caring demeanor toward others. And third, to walk humbly with your God captures the nature of a man's posture in relationship with God, and describes it as a dynamic, continuous progression, as in walking together.

Consider this scene of God walking in the garden with Adam, after creation and before the fall into sin. The Creator and His creation walk side by side, in relationship. Adam has no energy or power of his own making. God formed him from the dust! Adam does not and cannot generate life from within himself. God breathed the breath of life into Adam's nostrils so that he became a living being, and God also provides the sustaining life by which Adam lives and breathes every moment. This absolute and entire dependence upon the Creator for life is truth, and Adam's recognition and rest in that truth is his proper status, or posture, of humility toward God. Adam is humbly walking with God in the garden.

Mankind turned away from humility in the garden of Eden when the woman made the choice to embrace her Self-assessment of the tree and its fruit instead of God's instruction. When man abandoned his humility toward God, the void within filled with the poison of pride and the rule of Self. There is always only one authority on the throne of a man's heart, and *who* rules is clear by the fruit of his actions. Fallen man lives with Self on the throne and is a willing slave to fulfill Self's demands. This is original sin: the status of God being displaced by Self as the authority for man's life. Self is a brutal dictator, and mankind is powerless to dethrone Self.

So how can one be saved and restored to right relationship with God? Self cannot achieve, attain, or contribute in any manner to true redemption. In fact, Self has no interest in redemption. It is the rule of Self *from which* man is redeemed! The good news of redemption through Jesus taking our place in death on the cross is God's path to restore man's relationship with God and man's rightful posture of humility toward God. To be clear, there is only one narrow way of redemption. It is through Jesus!

> For by grace you have been saved through faith; and that not of your-
> selves, it is the gift of God; not as a result of works, so that no one
> may boast. For we are His workmanship, created in Christ Jesus for
> good works, which God prepared beforehand so that we would walk
> in them. (Ephesians 2:8-10)

When God, by His grace, grants faith to a man to believe in Christ's redemption, He also grants the power in Christ's name to deny and dethrone Self from the place of authority in one's life. Salvation by grace alone, through faith alone, and in Christ alone is the narrow and difficult way to salvation that Jesus speaks of in Matthew, saying:

> "Enter through the narrow gate; for the gate is wide and the way is broad that leads to destruction, and there are many who enter through it. For the gate is small and the way is narrow that leads to life, and there are few who find it." (Matthew 7:13-14)

The wide gate and broad path where most walk is deceptive and inviting. Self travels this path, and his favorite travel companion is the pride of life. The works and achievement of Self through doing better and working harder, reinforces the sin of pride and Self-rule. Any and every attempt of a man to claim credit for righteous behavior, or to gain favor from God by his acts, is a proclamation of Self-rule in the heart of man. Satan continues to whisper his lies and deceptions into a man's ears to reinforce and strengthen the pride of life in his Self-rule.

Remember Jesus' words in Luke 9:23, "If anyone wishes to come after me, he must deny [Self], and take up his cross daily and follow Me." Either Jesus is Lord, or Self is Lord in a man's life. It will never suffice to say words of submission to Christ's lordship, then act in submission to the lordship of Self. That is the height of hypocrisy and delusion. Those who delude themselves with a Self-driven works-based salvation will be stunned to hear the truth at the last judgement. Jesus describes this scene in Matthew 7.

> "Not everyone who says to Me, 'Lord, Lord,' will enter the kingdom of heaven, but the one who does the will of My Father who is in heaven will enter. Many will say to Me on that day, 'Lord, Lord, did we not prophesy in Your name, and in Your name cast out demons, and in Your name perform many miracles?' And then I will declare to them, 'I never knew you; leave Me, you who practice lawlessness.'" (Matthew 7:21-23)

When man denies Self, pride dies, and the posture of humility toward God is restored. It is only in humility that man can walk with God. Humility is the acknowledgement that God is Creator and man is His creation. God is everything, and as the created being, man is nothing except what His Creator wills. It is in knowing, accepting, and embracing this truth that man walks humbly with God and with his fellow man. In Philippians 2:3, we read, "Do nothing from selfishness or empty conceit, but with humility of mind regard one another as more important than yourselves." We have no greater model of humility than Jesus. Verses 5 through 8 point us to Jesus.

> Have this attitude in yourselves which was also in Christ Jesus, who, although He existed in the form of God, did not regard equality with God a thing to be grasped, but emptied Himself, taking the form of a bond-servant, and being made in the likeness of men. Being found in appearance as a man, He humbled himself by becoming obedient to the point of death, even death on a cross. (Philippians 2:5-8)

In Matthew 11:29, Jesus calls the Christian to "...learn from Me, for I am gentle and humble in heart, and you will find rest for your souls."

Consider how central the posture of humility toward others is in Jesus' teaching. In John 13, following the last supper, Jesus kneels to wash the feet of all the disciples, including Judas Iscariot, who Jesus knew would betray Him later that night. When He finishes, He tells them:

> "If I then, the Lord and the Teacher, washed your feet, you also ought to wash one another's feet. For I gave you an example that you also should do as I did to you." (John 13:14-15)

Jesus is straightforward in saying that the Christian man must walk humbly with his brothers. It is not possible to view your brother through selfish and prideful eyes and walk humbly with God at the same time. The inward posture of humility is universal to outward relationships; if the man has denied Self and pride, and has put on humility, you will see proof in his relationship toward God, his brothers, his family, neighbors, and strangers. In the same way, the posture of pride and Self is also universal in expression.

Walking humbly with God and with your brother will always happen together, as will loving God and loving your brother. We read from 1 John 4:20, "If someone says, 'I love God,' and hates his brother, he is a liar; for the one who does not love his brother whom he has seen, cannot love God whom he has not seen."

You are to walk humbly with God and your brother, loving your brother and God. This demonstration of perfect unity is the answer to Jesus' high priestly prayer to God the Father in John 17:

> "The glory which You have given Me I have given to them, that they may be one, just as We are one; I in them and You in Me, that they may be perfected in unity, so that the world may know that You sent Me, and loved them, even as You have loved Me." (John 17:22-23)

Humility shows the soft, receptive good soil of the heart is ready and able to receive the seed of God's word implanted. The seed then takes root and grows, bearing rich, bountiful fruit. Humility receives the word of God, which bears the fruit of transformation as we walk with God through life.

THE NARROW WAY OF HUMILITY

Ethan sat back in his chair, a look of certainty flooding his countenance. "This is a big concept for me to get my head around."

Jonathon nodded. "I sure understand what you're saying, Ethan. It is good to hear you acknowledge how significant this is. To be a follower of Jesus is all-encompassing of one's life and existence, and few will deny Self and surrender pride. There are knowers of Jesus, which is not the same as being a follower of Jesus. Knowers of Jesus like to be informed, but are unwilling to be transformed. They refuse to deny Self and pride, and to take on the posture of humility. That is the difficulty Jesus spoke of in Matthew 7:13-14, when He said, 'Enter through the narrow gate; for the gate is wide and the way is broad that leads to destruction, and there are many who enter through it. For the gate is small and the way is narrow that leads to life, and there are few who find it.'"

Ethan lifted his eyes from staring at the table and met Jonathon's steady gaze, saying, "Jonathon, I don't know *if* I can do this or *how* I can do this, but I know I want to follow Jesus."

Jonathon reassured Ethan, "The decision to deny Self and walk in humility may seem overwhelming, and on our own, it's impossible. But understand this; the posture of humility you take in recognizing God for who He is (your Creator), and in recognition of who you are (God's creature), *is* what dethrones Self in your life. The posture of humility determines the outcome of denying Self. This is the narrow way that leads to life – but we walk that narrow way together, and we will be there for each other to bring encouragement and even admonition when needed. And even more important than us walking together, we are walking humbly with God! We are not on our own on this journey, Ethan.

"In fact, that is what the gospel is all about. Where pride and sin separate and isolate man from a relationship with His God and Creator, redemption through Jesus restores that relationship. Because of redemption, Self and pride no longer rule, but they are like deposed scoundrels who skulk about and attempt to reimpose themselves through demands, desires, and fleshly appetites. That is why we must take up our cross daily! Next time, we need to talk about that throne from which Self was removed."

Discussion and Discipline

- Redemption and salvation for man is in Christ alone, by grace alone, through faith alone – it is the gift of God. How does recognizing this truth of scripture restore a man's natural posture of humility toward God, his Creator?

- What do you understand to be essential for "walking humbly with your God?" Are there things you must do? Are there things you must not do?

- In Philippians 2:5-8, the Bible describes how Christ "emptied Himself" and "humbled himself by becoming obedient to the point of death, even death on a cross." Have you recognized how central humility was to Jesus' mission and calling to provide a way of redemption to man?

- In Matthew 11:29, Jesus says to "learn from Me, for I am gentle and humble in heart, and you will find rest for your souls." In what ways did Jesus model humility for us, as He walked with His Father, and with the disciples and others? Why would Jesus say we will find rest when we learn about gentleness and humility from Him?

- God's redemptive plan is hard for man to accept. Why is this "gate" to life described by Jesus as small and this "way" to life seen as narrow and constricted? What makes this way so hard for a man to accept?

- Every attempt of a man to claim credit for righteous behavior, or to gain favor from God by his own acts, proclaims Self-rule and pride in the heart of man. This is not the gospel. Why does Jesus regard the "gate" as wide, and the "way" as broad, that leads to destruction?

Chapter Seven

The Kingdom of God

Christ Reigns Within!

The next week, Ethan and Jonathon met after breakfast at the trailhead of a hiking trail in a nearby state park. They had each packed a lunch and planned for their discussion and prayer time at the midpoint of the hike, where there was a rock outcropping which overlooked a broad valley with a wide, lazy river weaving through it.

Jonathon had shared with Ethan how he and Ethan's dad had agreed to encourage each other to stay active as they grew older, and they occasionally wove activities into their hours of meeting together over scripture and prayer. Hiking this trail was a favorite activity for them in the spring and summer months. He was glad when Ethan asked if they could do the same.

The early morning air was cool and crisp as they started the hike, but they warmed as the incline increased and the sun rose in the sky. After a bit, the trail widened so they could walk side-by-side, and Ethan began talking about the past week and his attention to issues with Self and pride each day.

"I'm listening to the things I say at home and at work. I'm hearing myself say things and then wishing I could take it back and say it differently. I hear my selfishness in response to Alicia's request for help with caring for Conner in the evenings. Inside I'm thinking, *'I've been working all day and I just need to relax'*. Another example is when a car squeezes into the freeway lane in front of me. I hear the voice of Self inside, screaming, *'Come on, stay in your own lane!'*

"Self tries to dictate when and with whom I connect at work. For instance, *'there's William. I'll walk down the other hallway, so I don't need to talk with him. That guy never stops yacking if you just say hi to him. I'm just too busy to waste time today.'* Sometimes it's clearly prideful or selfish, and other times I just don't know for sure.

Either way, I've thought a lot about the verse in James 1 that says, 'Everyone must be quick to hear, slow to speak, and slow to anger." (James 1:19).

"Ethan, that's wonderful insight; few men gain self-awareness about their own thoughts and attitudes," Jonathon encouraged Ethan. "That insight is an invaluable outcome of our daily practice of reading God's word and spending time in prayer. Both are essential to the Holy Spirit's process of transforming us by the renewing of our minds (Romans 12:2). We need to be alert to the schemes of Satan to distract and deceive us. Our adversary is always looking for opportunities to destroy and devour!"

Jonathon smiled as he said, "I remember when God first showed me how Self was reigning in areas of my life. I had a quick temper, and it would erupt when someone disagreed with my views and arguments. Your dad was the friend and brother who called me out on my Self-centered attitude and undisciplined emotions. I remember that first conversation like it was yesterday! He was incredibly humble and gentle when he asked me if I was aware of how my critical words and anger cut through others like a knife, wounding them and separating them from relationship with me."

"Whoa!" Ethan exclaimed, "My dad said that to you?"

"He sure did," Jonathon smiled as the picture of that day flashed through his mind. "It was one of the hardest days, but also one of the best days of our friendship. Proverbs 27:5-6 tells the truth when it says, 'Faithful are the wounds of a friend.' That day began a growing awareness of my need to deny and dethrone Self, and to take on a posture of humility toward God and others. That is the only effective antidote to the poison of pride."

Jonathon and Ethan walked into the clearing where the rock outcropping over-looked the valley below. There were picnic tables set up for hikers to rest and refuel for the remainder of their hike. They took their packs off, pulled their Bibles out and settled at one of the tables, giving their legs a much-needed rest. "Ethan," Jonathon said, "I'm not surprised to hear that God is teaching you and working in your life on these things. It's evidence that He is reigning in your heart and life, just as a king should. That is what I would like us to check out today in scripture. What happens with the throne in your life, when Self is denied and dethroned, and a man takes up his cross and follows Jesus?"

THE KINGDOM [THE REIGN] OF GOD

In John 18, Jesus stands as a prisoner before Pilate (John 18:33–37). Pilate had heard of Him. It was his responsibility to keep his ear to the ground, listening for rumblings of rebellion or insurrections among the Jews. There was no end to those who wanted and waited for a larger-than-life hero who would lead an uprising and overthrow the Roman occupiers. This hero, or Messiah, was front and center in Jewish folklore. The Old Testament prophets of Israel had foretold the event, when the Messiah would redeem God's people and restore the rule of the throne of David over the kingdom of Israel.

However, this seemed to be something different, and it was puzzling for Pilate. It was the Jewish leaders who had brought Jesus to him. They said Jesus claimed to be the Christ, a king, and they demanded that he be put to death. Pilate asked Jesus about this claim to be a king. Jesus seemed to affirm the charge, but then He said, "My kingdom is not of this realm" (John 18:36). What in the world is this kingdom, of which Jesus says He is king?

To understand the kingdom Jesus is talking about, we must be mindful of what happened in the beginning after God had placed man within His kingdom, the garden of Eden (Genesis 2, 3). We learn how the serpent infected man with the spiritual poison of pride, giving rise to Self within the heart of man. Self was lifted up to be like God, as man made the decision to rebel against God's reign and instead place Self on the throne of his life. This was treason against his loving, holy, and just Creator and God. Man was driven out of the garden, expelled from the kingdom where God had placed him to dwell in a relationship with Him (Genesis 3:23-24).

Reconciliation and restoration of man to a relationship with God could only be accomplished by an atonement which addressed all three components of His character: God is loving, holy, and just.

The atonement would be initiated by God's love for man. His holiness required a pure and sinless sacrifice. And that sacrifice would satisfy the demands of His perfect justice and wrath against sin. This atonement was accomplished by the sinless life and crucifixion of Jesus, God's Son, on the cross, and His resurrection demonstrated that death, sin, and the grave were conquered.

The virgin birth of Christ, His sinless life, His crucifixion, and His resurrection are central to God's plan for man's redemption, and cannot be overemphasized. Unfortunately, for many Christian men, this would be the limit of their knowledge of what the gospel and the work of Christ means for them. As you read the gospels of Matthew, Mark, Luke, and John, you discover Jesus spoke clearly and frequently of His mission from the Father. Yes, the culmination of His earthly ministry would be His substitutionary and sacrificial death on the cross for our sin, the atonement. But for those three years of His earthly ministry, everywhere He went, He preached the Kingdom of God. Throughout the four gospels, the Kingdom of God is referenced 85 times!

In Mark 1, John baptizes Jesus, and immediately afterward, Jesus spends forty days in the wilderness being tempted by Satan. He then comes into Galilee with a huge pronouncement. He was "preaching the gospel of God, and saying, 'The time is fulfilled, and the kingdom of God is at hand; repent and believe in the gospel'" (Mark 1:14-15).

We read in Luke 4 that Jesus preached in Capernaum, healing many and casting out demons. After teaching and performing many wonderful miracles, Jesus went and found a secluded place. However, "the crowds were searching for Him, and came to Him and tried to keep Him from going away from them. But He said to them, 'I must preach the kingdom of God to the other cities also, for I was sent for this purpose'" (Luke 4:42-44).

It is important to understand that the Jews were waiting for Christ, the king. It was prophesied the Christ would return to the throne of David to redeem Israel and throw off Israel's yoke of bondage. He would reestablish the kingdom to its prior glory under King David's reign. The picture in the minds of the people was of a great military or political leader and king. Now Jesus was preaching everywhere that the kingdom of God was at hand.

Many saw Jesus as a prophet of God, and this was big news! The Pharisees were questioning Jesus about this teaching, and they asked Him to be specific about when the kingdom of God was coming. His response made no sense to them! "He answered them and said, 'The kingdom of God is not coming with signs to be observed; nor will they say, Look, here it is! or There it is! For behold, the kingdom of God is in your midst'" (Luke 17:20-21). In this passage, the words "in your midst" are accurately translated as *within,* or *inside* you.

Jesus is challenging the picture in their minds, explaining that the kingdom of God is not a physical or geographical location, but that it is or will be *within* or inside man. To further clarify this new picture, we must understand the original word translated as the kingdom of God. This is the Greek word *basileia,* and its primary meaning in the first century was *"reign, rule, authority, sovereignty."* So, when we read the phrase kingdom of God in the Gospels, we should think in terms of God's reign, rule, authority, or sovereignty, *the reign, or rule of God.*

Jesus draws a new picture of what was prophesied. Redemption meant that atonement would be made for the sins of man, reconciling man back into a relationship with God, and the reign of God would come. He would be enthroned to reign within the hearts of men.

In another mind-bender for those stuck with the traditional picture of the political Messiah and the coming kingdom, Jesus tells Nicodemus that, "unless one is born again he cannot see the kingdom of God" (John 3:3). He also chides the disciples for rebuking those who were bringing their babies to be touched by Jesus, saying, "Permit the children to come to Me, and do not hinder them, for the kingdom of God belongs to such as these. Truly I say to you, whoever does not receive the kingdom [reign] of God like a child will not enter it at all" (Luke 18:15-17).

THE REIGN OF GOD, THE HOLY SPIRIT WITHIN

As He nears the end of His time of ministry, in Mark 9:1, Jesus was speaking to His followers, saying, "There are some of those who are standing here who will not taste death until they see the kingdom [the reign] of God after it has come with power." This must have been an intriguing thought to His disciples. They were still wrestling with the old earthly political kingdom picture they were taught in the synagogue!

Jesus tells them that He will ask the Father to give them the Holy Spirit, that will "be with you forever," and that "you know Him because He abides with you and will be in you" (John 14:16-17). Jesus assures them that "He (the Holy Spirit) will teach you all things" (John 14:26). Moreover, Jesus says the Holy Spirit will "guide you into all the truth" (John 16:13).

As the time for the atonement approaches, Jesus and His disciples travel to Jerusalem to celebrate the Passover. After the Passover meal, Jesus is betrayed by Judas to the chief priests and the elders of the people. They arrest Jesus, and cause him to be beaten and brutalized, and put on trial for blasphemy. Jesus is ultimately brought before the Roman governor of Judea, who gives the order for him to be executed by crucifixion. Jesus, God's pure and sinless atonement sacrifice, was crucified on the cross and was buried, and on the third day, He rose again from the dead. The Atonement and Resurrection were complete! Then we read in Acts 1,

> To these He also presented Himself alive after His suffering, by many convincing proofs, appearing to them over a period of forty days and speaking of the things concerning the kingdom [the reign] of God. (Acts 1:3)

Jesus preached the kingdom [the reign] of God for three years before the Atonement, and again preached the kingdom [the reign] of God during the forty days between the resurrection and the ascension.

And finally, in Acts 1:4-8, we read how Jesus commands them not to leave Jerusalem, but to wait for what the Father had promised. "'Which,' He said, 'you heard of from Me... you will receive power when the Holy Spirit has come upon you; and you shall be My witnesses both in Jerusalem, and in all Judea and Samaria, and even to the remotest part of the earth'" (Acts 1:4-8).

They obeyed Jesus and waited, and "When the day of Pentecost had come, they were all together in one place. And suddenly there came from heaven a noise like a violent rushing wind, and it filled the whole house where they were sitting. And there appeared to them tongues as of fire distributing themselves, and they rested on each one of them. And they were all filled with the Holy Spirit" (Acts 2:1-4). Jesus' promise in Mark 9:1 was fulfilled; many of those he was speaking with on that day did not see death before they saw the kingdom [the reign] of God come with power! The Holy Spirit, who was *with* them as Jesus taught throughout His ministry, was now *in* them, teaching them all things and guiding them into all the truth. This was the fullness of the promise of the kingdom [the reign] of God being established within the hearts of men.

This is the good news of the gospel! Full satisfaction for our sin has been made through the atonement of Jesus Christ, and now, through reconciliation, those who have been born again through faith in Jesus may receive the kingdom [the reign] of God in their hearts like children. This kingdom [the reign] of God is not like the original location of God's kingdom where He placed man in the garden of Eden to dwell in relationship with Him. God left the *place* of His glory, and went to where man was lost, to bring the kingdom of God to man. The reign of God is now to be established within the hearts of men!

As the humility of man is restored, and he recognizes his entire dependence upon God for life, redemption, and purpose, Self is dethroned and its dark kingdom of lies, speculation, and arrogance is to be destroyed. The throne in the heart of man does not remain empty after Self is cast down. Christ will now reign in the hearts of men as king, and He will reign in truth. This is the astounding "mystery which has been hidden from the past ages and generations, but has now been manifested to His saints, to whom God willed to make known what is the riches of the glory of this mystery among the Gentiles, which is Christ in you, the hope of glory" (Colossians 1:25-27).

WHO NOW REIGNS IN MY LIFE?

Jonathon and Ethan wrapped up their time of study and discussion, marveling at the brilliance, the beauty, and the mystery of God's redemption plan. How significant it was in redemption for the reign of God to be *within* or inside man, for Self to be deposed and for Christ to be enthroned in man's heart. This reign of God within made all the difference in the world for the efficacy of denying Self and turning from pride.

After their time of prayer together, Jonathon grinned, and asked if Ethan would mind if an old man caught a short catnap before starting the return trek back to the trailhead.

Ethan gave his approval and smiled as Jonathon stretched out in the grass off to the side of the rock outcropping, resting his head on his pack. For a moment, he could picture his dad doing the same thing, and a warm and soft sadness swept over Ethan as he remembered how much he loved times like this with his dad. Alongside the sadness was a growing appreciation for the time he had shared with his dad, and for the current treasure of friendship and time with Jonathon.

"*I guess this is how maturing and growing older feels,*" he thought. Then he offered a prayer of thanksgiving for God's rich blessings of family and friendship.

Looking out over the valley below, Ethan pondered this mystery from Colossians 1:27: "Christ in [me], the hope of glory." This new understanding of the reign of God amazed him! It seemed like big gaps in his understanding were being filled in and some of the critical questions he had were being answered. *Maybe this is the Holy Spirit teaching me, like Jesus said would happen.*

Three important questions seemed to be answered for him now. The first question was about being in charge, or ruling over his own life, versus denying Self: *Jesus said I must deny Self, but shouldn't I be in charge of my life, and be the one responsible and in authority over my stuff?* The answer to this question is: No! God did not create man with autonomy, or the capacity to be self-governed. That's why man's sin of pride and exulted Self was treasonous toward God, and humility was lost.

The second question had to do with the impossible task of denying Self: *How in the world can I work up enough willpower to deny Self and control my pride?* The simple answer to this question is found in the restoration of humility toward our Creator: In my own power or ability, I cannot be successful in this endeavor. In fact, *my* success would mean a return of Self to the throne of my life. But Christ now reigns within me! It is His power and authority under which I act daily. I am entirely dependent on God!

The third question was regarding concern for future encounters with this old problem of pride and Self: *How can I guard against pride and the re-establishment of Self on the throne of my life?* The answer to this question was also simple, but Ethan was certain the application would prove to be challenging: There is only one way to guard against pride. Humility, the continuous recognition of my entire dependence on God, is the only countermeasure to pride. The Bible's instruction in 1 Peter 5:5 to "clothe yourselves with humility," is a good word picture for a crucial daily spiritual reminder.

Ethan found he was experiencing an incredible inner peace and calm as he meditated on these truths from scripture. It was a peace that seemed impossible to explain or measure. He knew he was in God's presence, for Christ was reigning within him. Prayer was such a natural engagement in the closeness of this relationship, and he felt open and transparent as he prayed and worshipped while Jonathon rested.

Discussion and Discipline

- When Jesus preached the kingdom of God, He was not referring to a place or geographical location, but to the power and authority of the reign or rule of God, and that it is within you. How does that impact your understanding of the Christian life? What are some pictures in your mind about this that may need to be corrected?

- Men like to be in charge or in control (or, *Self* likes to be in control). How might this affect your willingness to recognize Christ as king in your daily walk? Are you ready to deny Self and follow Jesus?

- The Bible teaches that God created man in His image, and that man, as the creature, is entirely dependent on God. Man is not created to have autonomy or to be self-governed. On the other hand, humanism, or Self-worship (which encompasses every alternative theistic and atheistic thought system), believes everything starts and ends with man him*Self*, who is at the center of all existence and meaning. Many Christian men unwittingly attempt to straddle Christian doctrine and humanistic beliefs, trying to merge their need for atonement (Biblical truth) with their appetite for autonomy and control of their own life ("Self-rule"). Do you see how these contrasting belief systems are incompatible? How can you sort through and test what is truth and what is not truth?

- Paul said he would "rather boast about my weaknesses, so that the power of Christ may dwell in me" (2 Corinthians 12:9-10). Is it encouraging for you to know that if Christ reigns on the throne of your life (reflecting your entire dependence on God), it is His power and authority that you lean on to deal with pride and sin? Discuss an example of how that works in real life. What steps or actions do you take when you feel compelled to say or do something that would be from pride or Self?

SPIRITUAL WARFARE

Know the Enemy and the Battlefield

DDS Publishing

Chapter Eight

Spiritual Battles

Renewing the Mind

The next time Ethan and Jonathon met, they tried out a local coffee shop that had recently opened. The shop had a comfortable sitting room style, with groups of stuffed chairs and side tables that encouraged relaxed private conversation and multiple refills of the rich, hot beverages they served.

As they settled into a cozy set of chairs in the room's corner, Jonathon tossed a familiar quip to Ethan. "So how goes the battle, Ethan?"

Ethan smiled in response and said, "That's a great way to phrase the question, Jonathon. It really feels like a battle some days. What is difficult is figuring out exactly who the enemy is, and how to fight him! Alicia tells me she thinks I am my own worst enemy."

Jonathon gave a hearty laugh and said, "You've got a good wife, Ethan! There is actual truth to that statement for all of us. We have a spiritual enemy in Satan. The Bible often refers to Satan as our adversary. Now, we fight a lot of our battles on a very personal level. In fact, we fight them within our minds. Sometimes those battles start with the whispers of Satan, just like when he attacked Eve, asking, 'Has God said…?' (Genesis 3:1-5). He tempts us to question God's Word or His character, suggesting that we can't trust God, or that He may not love us because of our failures. Other times, we battle with lifelong patterns of thinking and old narratives that are deeply rooted in our way of looking at life. They often haunt our ability to build trusting relationships and live in humility toward others."

"How in the world are we supposed to fight that kind of battle, Jonathon?" Ethan's question revealed his concern and even some frustration. "I had hoped that with the reign of Christ within me, these sorts of struggles would at least diminish! But I gotta tell you, it almost seems to get more intense."

"I'm not surprised, Ethan," Jonathon tried to reassure him. "I think you are becoming more and more aware of those narratives and speculations than you ever were before. That makes sense, because we've been studying and discussing scripture together regularly for the past few months, and you've been faithfully keeping a time of daily devotions as well. You are becoming steadily more familiar with God's truth, and that is providing a strong contrast to the culture and lies of this world. Now you have a way to measure the old ways of thinking that are entrenched in your mind from years and even decades of training and practice. It's like slowly turning on a light brighter and brighter in a room where you've never actually seen how things look. Now things are really beginning to stand out to you!

"Your adversary, the devil, sees that you are growing in your faith and turning from your old ways. He will do anything to deceive and frustrate you from pressing forward in your walk with God. Let's dig into this today; we need to know how to navigate and maneuver on this battlefield."

KNOW THE ENEMY

As the Christian man walks through the conflicts of life, he may have misconceptions about those struggles. This makes it very difficult to know how to respond to the conflict effectively. He may think that he fights all spiritual battles directly against the devil and his demons, and they are always supernatural in scope and practice. Or, he may be ignorant of the forces of evil led by Satan (the devil) as the enemy who wishes to devour men. He may think he battles only against the temporal conflicts that he can see or act upon physically, or which he experiences within his own thoughts and emotions. Oblivious to the threat of evil, a man struggling through conflict assigns the responsibility for all his misfortune to fate, happenstance, or his own failings. It is important that our foundation for life rests squarely on the word of God, the Bible.

We can look to Ephesians to identify three enemies against which we must fight or resist:

> And you were dead in your trespasses and sins, in which you formerly
> walked according to the course of this world, according to the prince
> of the power of the air, of the spirit that is now working in the sons of
> disobedience. Among them we too all formerly lived in the lusts of our

flesh, indulging the desires of the flesh and of the mind, and were by nature children of wrath, even as the rest. (Ephesians 2:1-3)

Here we read that when we were dead in our trespasses and sins, we:

- Walked according to the course of this world,

- Walked according to the prince of the power of the air, and

- Lived in the lusts of our flesh, indulging the desires of the flesh and of the mind.

Our enemies are the world, the devil, and the flesh. The Christian man does not have the luxury of ignoring any of these three foes. The Holy Spirit teaches and equips the man who studies scripture and commits his way to God to resist temptations, to stand firm in testing, and to submit to God as his rock, salvation, and fortress. This is spiritual warfare!

THE DEVIL

Jesus referred to Satan as "the ruler of this world" (John 16:11). This is a sobering reality. We should be alert, not taken by surprise by unexpected adversity. 1 Peter 5:8 admonishes us to: "Be of sober spirit, be on the alert. Your adversary, the devil, prowls around like a roaring lion, seeking someone to devour." The devil hates mankind as the image bearer of God. It behooves us to consider how the enemy wages his war against the follower of Jesus, and to be alert to his deceptions and the weapons of destruction he employs against us.

Satan is not omnipresent; he can only be in one place at one time. He does, however, have a legion of demons to draw upon that test, torment, and deceive believers. Be aware that Satan bears no resemblance to the caricatured red devil with a pitchfork displayed in cartoons. He is genuinely beautiful; Ezekiel 28 describes him as "perfect in beauty" (Ezekiel 28:12). In 2 Corinthians, we are told that Satan "disguises himself as an angel of light" (2 Corinthians 11:13-15). He often presents his lies and destruction in desirable and attractive wrappings; they may even appear to be religious and upright.

THE COURSE OF THIS WORLD

The course of this world is a reference to the cultural values and norms which are embraced by the societies and people groups where one lives. These vary geographically, and fallen man forms, shapes, and practices them. They often land quite far from the mark of righteous actions and sometimes are contrary to them on the whole. The Christian man who follows Jesus and studies the Bible to increase his knowledge of God and His ways will become very familiar with acting counter-culturally in obedience to God. This can be difficult, as those around you question why you are not fitting in and acting in unison with them. This social pressure is a potent force for conformity, and the Christian man must know his Savior and stand firm on a Biblical foundation to resist the pressure. Romans 12 admonishes us to resist this conformity, and instead, to act decisively for transformation:

> And do not be conformed to this world, but be transformed by the
> renewing of your mind, so that you may prove what the will of God is,
> that which is good and acceptable and perfect. (Romans 12:2)

The choice before us is to conform or to be transformed! Conformity is clearly the easiest route; Jesus referred to this when He said, "the gate is wide and the way is broad that leads to destruction, and there are many who enter through it" (Matthew 7:13).

It is difficult to make the choice to swim against the tide of culture! Courage and strength are required to resist conformity to the world. They are forged in the crucible of reading scripture daily, spending regular time in prayer under the reign of God, and in fellowship with like-minded Christians. These disciplines are the bedrock of a man's spiritual formation over the years.

RENEWING THE MIND

We sometimes think of difficult circumstances as the way our adversary attempts to devour us. These may be hard situations in our family, other relationships, health, work, or finances. But in 2 Corinthians 10, the scripture gives us insight into a much different type of battlefield.

For though we walk in the flesh, we do not war according to the flesh, for the weapons of our warfare are not of the flesh, but divinely powerful for the destruction of fortresses. We are destroying speculations and every lofty thing raised up against the knowledge of God, and we are taking every thought captive to the obedience of Christ. (2 Corinthians 10:3-5)

The weapons we employ against the enemy are not of the flesh. They are not things we see and touch or hold in our hands, yet they are "divinely powerful for the destruction of fortresses." What are these fortresses in verse 4 that we are to destroy without physical weapons? The answer follows immediately in verse 5! We are to destroy "speculations and every lofty thing raised up against the knowledge of God."

A speculation is "the activity of guessing possible answers to a question without having enough information to be certain" (Speculation. (2024). https://dictionary. cambridge.org/us/dictionary/english/speculation). As Christian men, we know that God's word is truth, and it is unchanging and certain. Within God's word, the Bible, we learn and discover the knowledge of God. The spiritual battle we fight each day is "destroying speculations and every lofty thing" (fortresses) raised up against the knowledge of God, and taking "every thought captive to the obedience of Christ."

This battlefield is first in your own mind, among the narratives and habitual thought patterns which have been raised up as dark fortresses of wrong thinking. These fortresses oppose the truth revealed in the Bible as the knowledge of God.

We talk to ourselves all the time, often repeating ugly, shameful, and painful stories about our failures, sins, and shortfalls. As much as we need to practice being better listeners to others, we surely need to become better listeners of our own thoughts and self-talk. As we identify those repeating stories, they need to be measured against what the Bible says on the same topic. If we discover that the story is contrary to the knowledge of God, it is a speculation that we must destroy. The thoughts associated with that narrative must be taken captive and no longer be allowed to roam freely in our mind. This is a daily process of intentionality and discipline.

In Romans 12:2, this battlefield of the mind is identified as the determining factor in either being "conformed to this world, [or instead being] transformed by the renewing of your mind, so that you may prove what the will of God is, that which is good and acceptable and perfect."

As we destroy fortresses and take thoughts captive to the obedience of Christ (who now reigns within us), our lives are transformed. Satan is terrified of this outcome! The first battle of this kind resulted in the brokenness and depravity that has wreaked havoc on the world since then. That battle was fought and lost in Genesis 3. The battle began when the serpent whispered into Eve's ear, tempting her to question and evaluate God's clear and true word concerning the tree of the knowledge of good and evil (Genesis 3:1-6). Eve initially simply affirmed what God had said, with a small embellishment: "You shall not eat from it *or touch it*, or you will die." The serpent's next statement was to infer that God's word was not true and certain, saying, "You certainly will not die! For God knows that on the day you eat from it your eyes will be opened, and you will become like God, knowing good and evil."

Like a subtle tap against dominoes precariously balanced on the tabletop of eternity, the moment Eve entertained this thought which questioned God's clearly spoken word, a cascading destruction of innocence and humility was set into motion. Curious thoughts and information were the first push. They led to moments of intrigue that gave way to the heat of desire, which ignited the passions of temptation. As this process unfolded for Eve, the noxious seed of pride and Self implanted in her by the serpent germinated and sprouted. The final domino crashed to the ground as Eve acted; she ate from the tree of the knowledge of good and evil, and gave also to her husband, and he ate. Sin would now demand to be man's master.

Man had fallen from the natural and right place of the creature's uninhibited, transparent, and entirely dependent relationship with his Creator. Replacing the reign of God over man's life was the reign of Self through pride.

Now our adversary whispers lies to us through thoughts which question or speak contrary to the true knowledge of God. These thoughts build into repeated narratives which stand as fortresses of the enemy within our minds, challenging the knowledge of God in our life, pridefully demanding an answer to, "Has God really said...?" The only way to combat our enemy's lies and deception is to know and practice the truth given to us in the Bible.

When we have grown to know and recognize the truth, we can take each thought captive and measure every speculation against that truth. If the thought or speculation is false, we must destroy it and not allow it to occupy space in our minds again. This is how our minds are renewed, transforming our lives and our relationships with others by God's power and action through His Word.

THE KNOWLEDGE OF GOD IS TRUTH

Jonathon leaned forward as he said to Ethan, "Remember when you were struggling after your dad's death, thinking there was no hope, and you were feeling lost and alone? Those thoughts and feelings were speculations about the unknown future, and were lies about those who really care for you. The Bible is clear that in Christ you have a hope and future, and that Christ will never desert nor abandon you (Hebrews 13:5). We learned from scripture that those speculations of hopelessness were fortresses of the enemy that needed to be destroyed and the lying thoughts needed to be taken captive. We fight this battle in every area of our lives and relationships. Christ is on the throne now; He reigns in your life and brings His power and authority to bear with His word, as you identify those fortresses that need to be destroyed. Ethan, the truth, the Word of God, in which you have been growing, is shining the light in the darkness, and bringing to your attention those thoughts and 'every lofty thing raised up against the knowledge of God'" (2 Corinthians 10:5).

Ethan nodded his agreement with Jonathon, "This Christian life is not easy, is it? We really need to be ready and prepared for battle every day. I've heard guys say that being a Christian is just being a pansy. They have no idea! Jonathon, I'm so thankful to know that I have you praying for me! I know I need that."

"We're walking through this life together, Ethan – with God! You are never alone, my friend." Jonathon's reassuring tone gave strength to Ethan. "Let's take some time now to pray and ask God to continue His amazing transformative work in each of us through His word."

They prayed for each other, their families, and the church. It was humbling to acknowledge in prayer that these battles were difficult, and that they saw their entire dependence on God and His reign within them. It felt like the safest place to be. There is no better place or position to be than right where God created you to be: entirely dependent on Him!

Discussion and Discipline

- We are exhorted to be sober-minded and "on the alert" in 1 Peter 5:8-9, because the devil is prowling around like a lion, looking for someone to devour. He's watching you. Are you on the alert each day, watching for his lies and deception?

- Have you considered the concept from Romans 12:2 of being "transformed by the renewing of your mind"? How would you explain your understanding of having your mind renewed? What steps will you take to do this?

- In 2 Corinthians 6:16, Christians are described as "the temple of the living God," and God says that He will "dwell in them and walk among them." What does it mean to you that God dwells in you and wants to walk with you?

- In any type of conflict or battle, there is a great advantage to knowing your enemy. In Genesis 3, it is apparent that Eve does not recognize that her tempter is the enemy. She is taken in with the attractiveness of the possibilities he suggests, and becomes infected with pride, ignoring God's spoken truth and choosing another way. Do you recognize the enemy for who he is when he tempts you? Do you experience the same type of temptations as Eve experienced?

- Why is it significant that Satan is described in Ezekiel 28:12 as "perfect in beauty" and in 2 Corinthians 11:14, that he "disguises himself as an angel of light"? How might knowing this impact the way you consider your options in decision-making?

Chapter Nine

Self and Appetites

Disciplining the Appetites

E than leaned forward over the table as he asked Jonathon for his advice. "I really hope you might have some insight into an issue that's driving Alicia and me nuts!" he exclaimed. "We are pulling our hair out with Conner's behavior!"

Ethan had great respect for how Jonathon and his wife, Beverly, had raised their three now-adult children. They were not much younger than he was, so Ethan could watch how they grew through their childhood and teen years to become thriving Christian adults.

"What's up?" Jonathon took a sip of coffee as he leaned in to learn more.

"I had heard about the 'terrible twos' with kids, but I didn't think it was too bad with Conner. Now he turned four just a couple months ago, and I think the terrible part was just delayed until age four for him! He seems unable to sit still in church for even a minute, won't listen quietly to anything, and throws an absolute fit if we don't give him one of the three foods which he will eat for dinner. His behavior drives Alicia to tears, and she says it feels like Conner is running our household! What can we do?"

Jonathon chuckled for a moment, then apologized. "I'm sorry Ethan, I'm not making light of your frustration. I just remember that feeling you're describing, like it was yesterday. It really is a difficult time to struggle through with your child. It might help us look at the broader picture of mankind in general regarding what Conner is now experiencing as a child."

"What do you mean?" asked a puzzled Ethan.

Jonathon continued, "It sounds like Conner is going through a stage in development where he is discovering that he has activities, foods, and other things he prefers and enjoys more than other things. When he really likes something, he can't get enough of it, and just wants more. That makes sense, because engaging in that play, activity, or food creates genuine pleasure for him. The same is true for us as adults. There are activities and objects with which we experience a measurable amount of pleasure, and our impulse is to engage in more of those activities or objects.

The Bible uses the word "appetite" or "stomach" to address our pleasure-producing response to those things. The problem arises when that appetite is undisciplined and unrestrained, and it dictates a person's decisions and behavior. An uncontrolled appetite is devastating; Philippians 3 talks about those who worship their appetite.

APPETITE AND PLEASURE

Philippians 3 brings our attention to those who it described as, "Enemies of the cross of Christ, whose end is destruction, whose god is their appetite, and whose glory is in their shame, who set their minds on earthly things" (Philippians 3:17-19).

Paul, writing this letter to the church, identifies those who are enemies of the cross of Christ. This is a serious indictment! The cross of Christ – His substitutionary, sacrificial death for the reconciliation of sinful, Self-ruled man to God, is the means by which Self is dethroned and denied. The cross of Christ is the only way by which He redeems His followers and restores them to the natural posture of humility of the creature toward God, their Creator. Those who embrace the cross of Christ deny Self and take up their cross daily to follow Christ, and they enter the reign of God.

The man who loves and serves Self is an enemy of the cross of Christ. Self dictates his life and behavior, and his appetites are the primary governors which Self has appointed to rule over him. Appetites are those urges or delights which bring a sense of pleasure or enticement. We are most familiar with our appetite for food. It is our appetite which brings us back to the table multiple times per day, to satisfy or to feed it.

Having an appetite for something is not the concern, but serving that appetite as a god which then controls our decisions and overrules the instruction of scripture is idolatry. The Greek word that is translated as appetite is *koilia*, which refers to the *"belly, stomach, womb, etc.; by extension: the source of feelings and emotions"* (NIV Exhaustive Concordance Dictionary. Copyright © 2015 by Zondervan). When one is so captivated by the feelings which he experiences from a thing or activity in which he is engaged, he becomes enslaved to it.

We might immediately think of tangible things or behavior, like the abuse of substances, alcohol, narcotics, hallucinogens, etc. This is true, and we refer to the dependency (enslavement) of those in their grips as an addiction. But mankind also struggles spiritually with behaviors that are driven by Self and pride, which result in feelings of superiority and self-righteousness, or power and self-promotion. Romans 16 speaks of this, where it is written:

> Now I urge you, brothers and sisters, keep your eye on those who cause dissensions and hindrances contrary to the teaching which you learned, and turn away from them. For such men are slaves, not of our Lord Christ but of their own appetites; and by their smooth and flattering speech they deceive the hearts of the unsuspecting. (Romans 16:17-18)

Self trains a man to be motivated and even driven by his appetites. The world encourages this enslavement! Every promotion or product advertisement speaks to our appetites and attempts to stimulate the appetite to the point of purchase and consumption. It is dangerous and destructive to be enslaved to them; a man and those who care for him suffer greatly if he has uncontrolled appetites, and relationships are often destroyed.

Early in their children's lives, a parent loves and cares for their children by training them not to be enslaved to their burgeoning, or quickly growing, appetites. Instead, children are to be trained to listen to and respond to the instruction of their parents, overriding the compulsions and demands of their appetites. Proverbs 22:15 speaks directly to this very thought, saying, "Foolishness is bound up in the heart of a child; The rod of discipline will remove it far from him." This is difficult parenting, sometimes appropriately called tough love, and it is essential for the healthy development of the child and the future implications for their relationships with others in adult life. This builds and shapes a disciplined life, one that is not ruled by appetites, whims, and compulsions. Hebrews 12 describes the process and results of discipline for children and adults alike, saying: "For the moment, all discipline seems not to be pleasant, but painful; yet to those who have been trained by it, afterward it yields the peaceful fruit of righteousness" (Hebrews 12:11).

Even with good parenting, the foolishness which is bound up in the heart of a child may still not submit to the rod of discipline, and it remains defiant and insistent upon Self being enthroned. As an adult, the consequences of going astray from the socially and legally approved disciplines of behavior result in much more difficult and more painful consequences. Undisciplined and unrestrained appetites will consume and destroy a man! But there is still an opportunity to develop disciplines in one's life.

Success in developing those disciplines as an adult depends often upon a close and trusted relationship with a committed and frank-speaking friend who will provide accountability to the man. In the process of recovery from addiction appetites, this trusted friend is called a sponsor, and they are truthful and honest in the relationship. In other areas of overcoming enslavement to an appetite, this might be a pastor, counselor, or mentor. Personal friends are a wonderful source of support, but peers are often unable or unwilling to speak frankly and say the hard things. This is absolutely necessary to confront the person who is enslaved to his appetite and who is finding it difficult to dethrone this god they have been serving.

Above all, a posture of humility toward God, recognizing that He is your creator and that you are His creature, that He is everything, and you are only what He determines you to be through your life, is the most powerful and effective factor in dethroning and crucifying Self in one's daily life.

THE BLESSING OF DISCIPLINE

"Wow!" Ethan pondered the significance of parenting Conner and training him to control his appetites. "There are some serious consequences for Conner as an adult if Alicia and I don't get this right as parents while he is still so young. This is serious stuff!"

"You're right, Ethan," Jonathon encouraged him. "But you and Alicia are great parents; it can just feel overwhelming with how quickly children grow and change. It's easy to be surprised when new parenting challenges come up. Honestly, I feel like most of the heavy lifting in my parenting work happened on my knees in prayer!

"Beverly and I found ourselves at the end of our rope more than once, and we were constantly going back to God in prayer, and to others for support, when we felt clueless about how to handle things. Coming to the end of yourself and going to God in prayer is something we would all be better off doing sooner than later, whether it's with our parenting responsibilities or the things we wrestle with as adults."

"Jonathon, as an adult man now, can we talk about the appetites that I should control, and that I should take care not to allow them to get out of hand?"

"That's a great discussion for us to have, Ethan. Let's jump into that the next time we meet. Until then, I'll be looking forward to hearing how you and Alicia tackle the challenge of helping Conner with these new Self-control issues. Please, let Alicia know Beverly would welcome a phone call if she would like some reassuring 'Mom' support!"

Discussion and Discipline

- Have you been able to recognize times when you were tempted or tested by the world, the devil, or your flesh? How did you resist or refuse the temptation?

- Everyone has areas where they have difficulty saying "No" to their appetite. When does that struggle turn into the appetite becoming your god, and you becoming "an enemy of the cross of Christ"?

- There are appetites of the flesh which seem more obvious: food, drink, comfort, sexual and other pleasures. Paul also speaks of appetites or desires of the mind: greed, power, lust, revenge, etc. What appetites are the most difficult for you to manage, or to keep under control?

- How would being trained in discipline as a child have reduced the difficulty of facing and dealing with your appetites as an adult? If you are a parent with a young child who needs discipline, are you willing to provide what they need? For many parents, Self will not allow them to act toward their child in a way that causes the child to not like them. Is this a problem? Describe why.

Chapter Ten

The Lust of the Flesh

Self - On the Throne or On a Cross

There was a spring in his step as Ethan entered the restaurant where he was meeting Jonathon for breakfast. He was feeling hopeful and encouraged by the progress made in parenting Conner through this new phase of tantrums and defiant behavior. There was still a long way to go, but even after just a week, he was seeing good indications that Conner's response to their discipline was already improving. This was a tremendous relief for both him and Alicia.

"Good morning, Ethan!" Jonathon smiled as Ethan slid into the booth across from him. "You look like you've had a good start to the day."

"I have had a good start, Jonathon! Alicia got some great ideas from Beverly about how to work through Conner's belligerence, and we're already seeing some improvements. I can't tell you how thankful I am for both you and Beverly!"

"You're welcome, Ethan. I'm sure there's a way to go yet, but it's great to hear that things are moving in the right direction. The flesh has a powerfully strong appetite, and it requires firm, consistent responses to control it. Even for a young child!"

"Speaking of a strong appetite, I'm sure ready for breakfast," Ethan quipped.

The men ordered their breakfast and picked up on their previous discussion, dealing with the appetites which need to be controlled as an adult man.

APPETITES OF THE FLESH

In the book of 1 John, chapter 2, we read:

> Do not love the world nor the things in the world. If anyone loves the
> world, the love of the Father is not in him. For all that is in the world,
> the lust of the flesh and the lust of the eyes and the boastful pride of
> life, is not from the Father, but is from the world. (1 John 2:15-16)

This provides us with a summary of the three broad areas of appetite which will wreak havoc if a man allows them to have a foothold in his life: the lust of the flesh, the lust of the eyes, and the boastful pride of life. The Greek word for lust here is *epithymia*; it is translated as *"desire, longing (in contexts where the desire is positive and proper); coveting, craving, lusting (in contexts where the desire is immoral and sinful)" (NIV Exhaustive Concordance Dictionary. Copyright © 2015 by Zondervan).*

We also see that each of these areas of appetite was triggered by the newly elevated Self in Genesis 3:6, when the woman was tempted by the serpent.

> When the woman saw that the tree was good for food [the lust of the
> flesh], and that it was a delight to the eyes [the lust of the eyes], and that
> the tree was desirable to make one wise [the boastful pride of life], she
> took from its fruit and ate... (Genesis 3:6)

The appetites, or lusts of the flesh, are those impulses which, if acted on, promise to bring pleasure or enticement to our physical body, or would stimulate chemical activity to stimulate pleasure in the brain. In either case, the impulse or appetite may appear suddenly or be especially urgent. This differs from an appropriate sense of hunger. Regarding food, for example, your body grows hungry each day as caloric reserves from previous meals are depleted, and your body lets you know you should eat food by feeling hungry. As you then eat something, the feeling of hunger dissipates and goes away.

However, you may eat food that is very pleasurable in your mouth by the way it tastes, and even after your hunger has disappeared completely, your appetite, or lust for that food, demands that you continue eating for the sheer pleasure of taste. Just a short time later you may think, *"I can't believe I ate that entire bag of potato chips; I feel sick to my stomach now!"* This would be an example of serving your appetite as a god (Philippians 3:17-19), or being enslaved by your appetite (Romans 16:17-18). This type of enslavement to appetites causes one to be filled with a sense of regret and disappointment in themselves. It feels shameful to be out of control and unable to resist one's appetite.

A WARNING!

When commandeered and distorted by Self, man's appetites can be a demanding voice in a man's thoughts, coercing him to kneel at the altar of lust and serve this ruthless tyrant. Behind the curtain of every demanding lust is the uncrucified Self pulling the levers as it strives to return to the throne of a man's life. Self has a motivated ally in Satan, as he prowls about the earth looking for someone to devour (1 Peter 5:8), whispering his lies and deception in the ears of men, trying to separate them from God.

The momentary pleasure of feeding those appetites is a powerful influence on the man, even when he knows that sin pushes him away from his gracious God. He might, for a short or lengthy period, be determined to fight against the lusts of the flesh, mustering all his strength of will and motivation to turn a deaf ear to the demands of his appetites. Please hear and understand that this tremendous effort and act of will is performed under the strength and ability of the Self! It is like a man standing inside a large bucket and exerting all his strength to grasp the rim of the bucket and lift himself up.

Self is utterly powerless to bring atonement, redemption, reconciliation, or sanctification for the life of a man. Yet, some men struggle in this manner for years, seeing no other avenue toward freedom while being determined to live rightly. Several succumb to hopelessness and remain lost without a way forward. The most troubling outcome is for some men who choose resignation to the enslavement to appetites while believing they are also following Jesus. They think they can live lives with dual kingship, that they can divide their lives into two realms. They want to allow Self to remain on its throne, ruling over the temporal realm, while they install a duplicate throne alongside Self's throne for their Self-defined Jesus to rule over the "spiritual" realm of their lives.

This might look like the "party at the bar on Friday night" and then "worship Jesus in church on Sunday" guy. This is heresy. It is a Self-made religion which conjures up a toothless, cardboard "Jesus" made to suit their pleasure. All the while, behind the curtain in this fantasy dual-rule realm sits a fortified and empowered Self upon the one and only real throne of the man's life. From this place, Self stirs up and ignites the lusty appetites to enslave each man, knowing the resulting shame will drive the man deeper and deeper into hiding when he hears God walking in the garden.

Continuous separation of the man from God is the ultimate aim of Self. Because of its great deception, this is perhaps the most tragic of the failed outcomes regarding appetites. Flee from such a deception when the devil whispers this devious suggestion into your ears, hoping he can capitalize on the difficult struggles of walking the narrow way as you follow Christ.

Jesus pulled no punches when He laid out the path for those who wished to come after Him: "And He was saying to them all, 'If anyone wishes to come after Me, he must deny [Self], and take up his cross daily and follow Me'" (Luke 9:23).

Jesus Christ stands boldly and unequivocally opposed to the scoundrel Self who separates you from God. He rescues those who wish to be set free from its bondage and enslavement, empowering them to deny/dethrone Self and send him to crucifixion daily. When Self is on the cross along with pride, and the reign of God is received as a child, the return of humility to the heart of man understands and acknowledges the truth that God is everything. Humility, the place of entire dependence on God, concedes and submits that each moment of life and every potent act of the man is God's work and action, and by His authority alone. This is the only viable path to freedom from enslavement to lusts of the flesh and the eyes and the boastful pride of life.

HOW DOES GOD FREE ME FROM ENSLAVEMENT TO MY APPETITES?

There is a popular internet video of a shepherd who rescues his sheep from a long, narrow trench dug across the pasture. The shepherd, with great effort, pulls the sheep up and out of the trench where it had been helplessly trapped. The sheep leaps to its feet, running and jumping with exhilaration at being set free. After excitedly bounding about in a circle a few times, the sheep promptly runs and falls once again into the same trench... as the shepherd watches and shakes his head. Here is the point: Our Great Shepherd is the only one who can rescue and free us from enslavement to other things. This is accomplished through Christ's sacrifice on the cross on our behalf; when we believe on Jesus, we are born again with a new nature. We are new creations in Christ (2 Corinthians 5:17) and sin shall not be master over us, for we are not under law but under grace (Romans 6:14). But we would be wise to stop blindly and stupidly running back into the same traps which the devil has laid out before us. These traps are quite easy to see when we know what to look for and we are motivated by our love for Christ to do so.

KNOW THE TRUTH OF WHAT LUST IS AND DOES

The first step is to know and embrace the truth in scripture, and from scripture, to see the lust for what it is and does. Our source of truth is God's written word, the Bible. We need to read and study it as a daily habit. We must avail ourselves of the gifts that Jesus has given to the church in pastors, teachers, and others, who are specifically gifted to explain to us the word of God accurately (Ephesians 4:11-16). From the Bible, we can know clearly what lust is, what it looks like, and the damage and pain it causes a man. By knowing the truth, we can call out the lies and deception of Self and Satan, which would lead us to jump right back into those traps of sin. The truth about lustful appetites is clear in scripture. Regarding sexual lust, in Matthew 5, Jesus said: "You have heard that it was said, 'You shall not commit adultery; but I say to you that everyone who looks at a woman with lust for her has already committed adultery with her in his heart" (Matthew 5:27-28).

There is no difference between engaging in lustful thoughts about a woman and engaging in the physical act of fornication or adultery with her. We also read in 1 John 3:15 that "Everyone who hates his brother is a murderer; and you know that no murderer has eternal life abiding in him." The lust of hate toward another man is equivalent to murdering him! Lust is not a "lesser" sin! If a man hears that thought whispered into his ear, it is the deceptive voice of the devil, singing the same song he sang to Eve.

The apostle Paul, writing to the church in Colossae, did not pull any punches in addressing lustful appetites, saying,

> Therefore consider the members of your earthly body as dead to immorality, impurity, passion, evil desire, and greed, which amounts to idolatry. For it is because of these things that the wrath of God will come upon the sons of disobedience. (Colossians 3:5-6)

First, he admonished the church to consider their body as dead to them. Immorality, impurity, passion, evil desire, and greed are all lusts of the flesh. He instructed men that their compulsion toward any of these lusts should be as much as a corpse would respond to food. Paul warned these lusts will cause the wrath of God to fall upon people, those called the "sons of disobedience." God is filled with wrath toward unrestrained lustful appetites.

Knowing the truth about lustful appetites equips a man to recognize the lies about them, and he understands the real consequences of engaging with them. We spoke of how the devil lies about sexual lust, saying that *it is not actually having sex with the woman,* as if lust were a lesser sin than adultery. That is a lie meant to diminish the significance of lust. Another lie about lustful appetites is, *no one else will ever know about your thoughts, so it's like nothing really happens.* Do you understand God is omnipresent, with you at all times, and omniscient, knowing your every thought, impulse, word, and action?

The consequences of being enslaved to lustful appetites are severe and manifold. They include detrimental physical impact on the body, the destruction of relationships, the overwhelming guilt and shame on the soul and mind, and ultimately, the unleashed wrath of God upon the man who is separated from Him and instead serves the god of his appetites.

This should sound familiar to us; we are describing spiritual warfare, refusing to be conformed to the world and instead being transformed by the renewing of our minds (Romans 12:1-2). We need our minds to be renewed regarding lustful appetites, to learn the truth about them according to scripture. We can then destroy speculations and lofty things raised up against the knowledge of God (fortresses) by measuring the lies and false narratives about lustful appetites against the truth of scripture. Every thought must be taken captive to the obedience of Christ (2 Corinthians 10:3-5). From scripture, we also renew and train our mind on how we are then to live and be in relationship with others. This transformation by renewing our mind is essential for truth to grow and bear the fruit of righteousness in our lives.

CONSIDER HOW YOU WILL RESPOND TO THE TRUTH

The second step is to consider and determine our plan of action. How we will respond to lust when we identify it. This is critical! It's like practicing a fire drill before there is the stress and intensity of an actual fire. It gives you the opportunity to decide how you will respond in a situation without the stress, feelings, or anxiety that will be present when it actually happens. The stress, feelings, and anxiety make it extremely difficult to think clearly and make a wise decision. So we must decide ahead of time and practice our plan of action! Here are some examples of lust traps and action plans:

Lust Trap	Action Plan
Sensual images appear on an internet page.	Close that browser tab immediately. Use Family Safety tools on your device!
Unhealthy fast foods, candy, and treats are everywhere.	Immediately grab an alternative (carrot, mint, coffee). Keep them out of your home!
A coworker flirts with you, or makes suggestive comments.	Talk about your wife. Talk about your faith. Leave the room!
Sensual images appear in a movie or on a TV advertisement	Immediately change the channel. Leave the movie theater!

Review and examine past occasions of temptation and your behavior. Be honest with yourself about those things which stir up lustful desires within you. Identifying those lustful appetites is the first necessary step. Then decide on your action plan for when those temptations present themselves. Whichever areas of lust temptations are most dangerous for you, talk through your action plans with another trusted Christian man. This practice is incredibly helpful for avoiding the lust traps Satan is certainly going to be placing before you.

Returning to 1 John, we learn another critical truth: There is no middle ground or compromise possible that allows a man to love lustful appetites AND have the love of the Father in him. We are told,

> Do not love the world nor the things in the world. If anyone loves the world, the love of the Father is not in him. For all that is in the world, the lust of the flesh and the lust of the eyes and the boastful pride of life, is not from the Father, but is from the world. (1 John 2:15-16)

Until you know and understand the truth about lustful appetites, you will believe the lies told to you about them, and you will love them. Only after knowing the truth, being transformed by the renewing of your mind, and seeing lustful appetites for what they really are, can you possibly choose *not* to love them!

CHRIST ALONE FOR SALVATION FROM ENSLAVEMENT TO SIN

In humility, a man can turn only to Christ for salvation and rescue from enslavement to sin. As Christ reigns within, and lives through the man, the man walks forward in obedience to his Creator on the narrow way of following Jesus. This may seem simple, but it is certainly not easy, or without pain or loss.

This is the most fundamental truth which will determine whether a man will remain enslaved by lustful appetites, or if he will be rescued from his chains. If lustful appetites are enslaving the man, Self is on the throne of his life. Self, the outgrowth of man's treasonous pride and defiance toward God, is that which ignites and fans the fiery cravings of every lustful appetite, whether it be gluttony for food, illicit sexual desire, or greed for possessions and power.

It is easy to understand why Self cannot be enlisted to wage war against lustful appetites. It would be like trying to extinguish the flames of a raging fire by dousing it with gasoline! Self and its pride are the very reason lustful appetites are such a trouble for man. That is why Jesus told us that Self must be denied and a man must take up his cross daily and follow Him. Self is either on a throne or on a cross! The Bible reiterates this necessity of Self being crucified.

> For if we have become united with Him [Christ] in the likeness of His death, certainly we shall also be in the likeness of His resurrection, knowing this, that our old self was crucified with Him, in order that our body of sin might be done away with, so that we would no longer be slaves to sin; for he who has died is freed from sin. (Romans 6:5-7)

> Even so consider yourselves to be dead to sin, but alive to God in Christ Jesus. Therefore do not let sin reign in your mortal body so that you obey its lusts, and do not go on presenting the members of your body to sin as instruments of unrighteousness; but present yourselves to God as those alive from the dead, and your members as instruments of righteousness to God. (Romans 6:11-13)

The man who wishes to be set free from enslavement to pornography, sexual lust, alcohol, drugs, gluttony, the thirst for power, or any other lustful appetite, must deny Self, and place it on the cross daily as he follows Christ. This is concurrent with receiving the reign of God within by confession of faith in Christ alone, by grace alone. In this way, we are united with Christ in the likeness of His death (our old Self was crucified with Him) so that we would no longer be slaves to sin.

WALK FORWARD WITH CHRIST ON THE NARROW WAY

Paul details the terrible struggle within the man who knows and understands the law of God, but sees he is a prisoner to the law of sin and death through the lustful appetites of the flesh in Romans 7. He summarizes this struggle in verses 22-23, where he says, "For I joyfully concur with the law of God in the inner man, but I see a different law in the members of my body, waging war against the law of my mind and making me a prisoner of the law of sin which is in my members."

Following that summary, in verse 24, he makes a mournful lament, with a painful plea for help, "Wretched man that I am! Who will set me free from the body of this death?" This cry of desperation is answered immediately with this joyful shout, "Thanks be to God through Jesus Christ our Lord!" From there, starting with the second half of Romans 7:25 through chapter 8:4, he explains that what the Law of Moses could never accomplish, "God did: sending His own Son in the likeness of sinful flesh and as an offering for sin, He condemned sin in the flesh, so that the requirement of the Law might be fulfilled in us, who do not walk according to the flesh but according to the Spirit."

This is the gospel! What could not be accomplished through the law, and what man could not achieve through Self or in his own effort by trying harder or working more, *God did, through Christ!* The gospel is always the solution to the problem which is troubling you. The following verses, Romans 8:5-9, present the contrast which is at the crux of this wretched place of conflict for the man who would choose to follow Jesus:

> For those who are according to the flesh set their minds on the things of the flesh, but those who are according to the Spirit, the things of the Spirit. For the mind set on the flesh is death, but the mind set on the Spirit is life and peace, because the mind set on the flesh is hostile

toward God; for it does not subject itself to the law of God, for it is not even able to do so, and those who are in the flesh cannot please God. However, you are not in the flesh but in the Spirit, if indeed the Spirit of God dwells in you. But if anyone does not have the Spirit of Christ, he does not belong to Him. (Romans 8:5-9)

In this passage, there are two conditions, or states of being, described for a man, and each has a unique outcome. It reflects the decision which Jesus said each man must make; if you wish to follow Him, you must deny Self. This passage in Romans describes those who follow Self and those who follow Christ. What differentiates each state of being and its outcome is the action associated with it. The following table illustrates the action and the resulting outcome from the passage.

	Those who follow Self	Those who follow Christ
State of being	Those who are according to the flesh.	Those who are according to the Spirit.
Action	Those who set their minds on the things of the flesh.	Those who set their minds on the things of the Spirit.
Outcome	Death.	Life and Peace.

Those who are according to the Spirit set their minds on the things of the Spirit. This is the transformed life spoken of in Romans 12:1-2. It has not conformed to the world, but is transformed by the renewing of the mind. This calls for a continuous recognition of one's entire dependence on God (humility), and results in a mindset of praying at all times and being led by the Spirit of God.

A consistent and regular diet of consuming the truth of God's word is essential to identifying the speculations and lofty things in your mind that need to be destroyed. This is following Jesus, walking with Him on the narrow way – "For all who are being led by the Spirit of God, these are sons of God" (Romans 8:14).

LOST OPPORTUNITIES

Ethan was saddened as he thought back to his high school years. He remembered friends from junior high who became distant in high school as they made choices for activities and recreation. Several former playground buddies of his became known as real party animals by their senior year. He knew at least two of them who still lived locally, and alcohol and wild behavior destroyed their lives. They had dropped out of college before completing even one year and hadn't been able to hold a steady job since.

"Those lustful appetites are brutal," he said. "I've seen how they can absolutely wreck lives!"

"Yes they are," Jonathon agreed. "They're nothing to experiment with. The problem is that Self is so incredibly confident and cocky. It makes teenagers and young adults feel like they are indestructible. Just like with Eve in the garden of Eden, pride continues as the poisonous concoction that fuels Self, refuses to hear and be guided by wisdom, and destroys relationships with others. Next week we can talk about the lust of the eyes a bit, looking at how that's similar, but different, from the lust of the flesh. Then, two weeks from now, we'll hit the third area identified in 1 John 2:16, the boastful pride of life."

Discussion and Discipline

- 1 John 2:15-16 says, "Do not love the world nor the things in the world. If anyone loves the world, the love of the Father is not in him. For all that is in the world, the lust of the flesh and the lust of the eyes and the boastful pride of life, is not from the Father, but is from the world." This is an either/or truth; either the love of the world is in you, or the love of the Father is in you. The answer to "Which one is in you?" is determined by your thoughts and behavior. What do your thoughts and behavior reveal?

- Have you experienced the frustration and exhaustion of attempting to control the appetites of the flesh by Self, employing your own will or strength? Can you relate to the struggle described in Romans 7?

- When Self is tempting you with a lustful appetite for something, all you think about is the pleasure and satisfaction which is associated with it for a brief time. Can you see how powerful and necessary it is to learn the truth from scripture about the destruction that also is associated with the same lustful appetite? Are you willing to learn and tell yourself the truth about that appetite from scripture?

- The first step in throwing off the enslavement to lustful appetites is to decide not to love them anymore (1 John 2:15). This happens as you open your eyes to the truth about them from scripture, and compare that with the lies told to you by Self and the devil. Being transformed by renewing your mind with truth is an essential outcome of walking the narrow way with Jesus. What are some ways your mind has been renewed? What do you now know is true, and have you destroyed the fortresses (speculations) and lofty things raised up against that truth? What are some ways you know that your mind may still need to be renewed?

Chapter Eleven

The Lust of the Eyes

The Lamp of the Body

J onathon paused as the waitress walked up to take their order.

"Will it be the usual this morning, gentlemen? You know, you're both kind of predictable!" Sandra flashed her bright smile and tilted her head to one side with a playful look. She worked most Saturday mornings when Ethan and Jonathon met for breakfast, and she had a knack for remembering what all the regular customers ordered. Her skills as a server were exceptional, and she discovered many years ago that flirting with the men led to increased tips. She was a very attractive woman and caused more than a few men to blush with the attention she gave to them as customers.

"Sounds good for me, Sandra," Jonathon smiled back as he waved off the menu she was offering. "You make this pretty easy with your splendid memory!"

"Same here," Ethan laughed, "except I'll take some cream for my coffee today. I don't want to be too predictable!"

Sandra's laughter spilled over them as she poured the coffee she had brought with her to the table. After pouring the coffee, she promised to return with cream, then turned and glided across the dining room toward the kitchen.

Jonathon's smile faded a bit as he saw Ethan's eyes following Sandra across the room. He knew Ethan's character, that he would never consider being unfaithful to Alicia. But he also knew that Satan would capitalize on the slightest opportunity to destroy a Christian man and his family, through even the most insignificant of missteps.

Ethan turned his attention back to the table and noticed Jonathon's eyes on his. Embarrassed, he glanced down at the coffee cup in his hands.

"Ethan, it's been great hearing how you and Alicia, as parents, are caring for and training Conner to control his appetites at a young age, before he and those appetites get to a size that's not so manageable. Last time we met, we looked at what the Bible says about our adult appetites, and how they need to be controlled as well. In 1 John 2, we looked at the lusts of the flesh, and learned how we need to take up our cross daily so Self is crucified. Today we planned to look at the second area, the lust of the eyes."

THE LAMP OF THE BODY

God designed the eyes of mankind remarkably! We read in Matthew 6,

> "The eye is the lamp of the body; so then, if your eye is clear, your whole
> body will be full of light. But if your eye is bad, your whole body will
> be full of darkness. So if the light that is in you is darkness, how great
> is the darkness!" (Matthew 6:22-23)

Some have read Jesus' words here and correlated them with the folksy saying that "the eyes are the window to the soul," which infers that the eyes are just a neutral portal, or a window, through which one can gaze, and see into the soul and understand its condition or state. But this is not true! We cannot see through another's eyes and know what is within. The scripture says, "For who among men knows the thoughts of a man except the spirit of the man which is in him" (1 Corinthians 2:11)?

To think we know the thoughts or what is within another person is a prideful speculation. Our only view of another is seeing the fruit of their actions or their behavior. Jesus addresses this truth in Matthew 7, saying, "You will *know* them by their fruits (Matthew 7:16-20). In this passage, the Greek word *"epiginōskō"*, translated as *know*, means *"to recognize, or come to understand them."*

That is why the imagery in Jesus' words, "the eye is the *lamp* of the body," is a very important picture to understand. Looking at the original Greek language of these verses helps to clarify that *eye* (*ophthalmos*) means the physical eye, and *lamp* (*lychnos*) refers to a clay or metal lamp filled with oil, with a wick to light. "If the eye is clear" (*haplous*) refers to good health, or healthy, and "if the eye is bad" (*ponēros*) means unhealthy, wicked, or opposed to God and His goodness. Jesus is not saying the eyes allow you to see what is inside the person, but He is saying the eyes, like a lamp, *will determine the resulting condition within the man.* If the eyes are clear/healthy, they will fill the person with light. If the eyes are bad/unhealthy, they will cast darkness within the person.

In Matthew 6, Jesus is focusing on the individual man's practices, including giving to the poor, prayer, fasting, and storing up treasures. Following this statement on the eye, Jesus clarifies it is impossible for a man to serve two masters, and then instructs us not to be anxious for the needs of our life, but to seek first His kingdom and His righteousness. This context clarifies that Jesus is saying each man *is responsible for his eyes,* to discipline and train his eyes to keep them clear and healthy. What the man allows his eyes to take in, or to be fixed upon, determines whether they are clear or bad, which then determines if the eye radiates either light or darkness within the man.

There is a strong correlation between the lustful appetites of the eyes and the lustful appetites of the flesh. Often, the lust of the eyes triggers or inflames the lusts of the flesh. Consider why a business may pay as much as 100 times more for a television ad than they would pay for a radio ad. The visual component of television is much more effective for advertising products like food, fashion, or luxury items. These are items which affect emotion, desire, or impulse. What the eyes see is directly connected within your brain to conscious thoughts and subconscious reactions to the world around you. There is an immediate connection between what the eyes see and a reactive thought outcome.

TREASURE THE WORD OF GOD

The most critical element of defense for a man to protect his integrity and to guard his heart is to build a solid fortress for all of his life with God's word. Psalm 119 speaks to this, saying, "Your word I have treasured in my heart, that I may not sin against You." The man who treasures, or stores up God's word in his heart, has laid a solid wall of truth defense against the lies and lusts of the eyes and the flesh. Remember that the renewing of the mind depends upon having the truth of God's word at the ready for evaluating and measuring the speculations and lies of the world, the flesh, and the devil, and then destroying them.

> How can a young man keep his way pure? By keeping it according to Your word. With all my heart I have sought You; do not let me wander from Your commandments. Your word I have treasured in my heart, that I may not sin against You. (Psalm 119:9-11)

BE ON THE ALERT

The next step of defense for a man against the lust of the eyes is to be alert and sober-minded. The most prolific area of testing for men is sexual in nature, and only the most naïve or simple-minded man is unaware that any moment of the day may bring before him a testing for lust of the eyes. Jesus affirms this, specifically calling out the lust of the eyes when He says, "But I say to you that everyone who looks at a woman with lust for her has already committed adultery with her in his heart" (Matthew 5:28). The Christian man is admonished in scripture to, "Be on the alert, stand firm in the faith, act like men, be strong" (1 Corinthians 16:13).

In Ephesians 6:10-18, the Christian is admonished to "Be strong in the Lord and in the strength of His might," and to take up the full armor of God so that you will be able to resist in the evil day, to stand firm. The apostle also writes that we are to "Be on the alert with all perseverance." Finally, in 1 Peter 5:8, we are instructed to, "Be of sober spirit, be on the alert. Your adversary, the devil, prowls around like a roaring lion, seeking someone to devour."

Being alert and sober-minded at all times is the mindset of a warrior. It is wise to take on the mindset of a warrior, knowing that your adversary is looking for you to devour you.

TURN YOUR EYES

The next defense against the lust of the eyes is a trained discipline to immediately turn the eyes away when the appetites are triggered. Each time the testing for lust presents itself, the alert Christian man turns his eyes away, giving no provision for the lusts of the eyes or the flesh (Romans 13:14). Let me speak bluntly to every man on this. Satan's favorite lie with which he entices a man is to suggest that the man can simply "appreciate" and linger on a woman's physical beauty without thinking lustful thoughts or arousing lustful appetites. It is foolishness for a man to hesitate in turning away his eyes for even a second, for the barbed hooks of the devil's bait set themselves into a man's thoughts and flesh without warning.

Being on the alert means a man is ready to take instant action in response to the enemy's movements. This disciplined warrior response needs to be practiced and trained in a man, over and over and over again. Then he must follow his action plan every time.

TAKE EVERY THOUGHT CAPTIVE

At the same time a man is quickly turning his eyes away, he must also consistently police his mind and take every thought captive, measuring it against the truth of God. This practice is an essential element of the process of renewing your mind, which is life transforming for a man (Romans 12:1-2). How does this actually look? To say it plainly, you talk to yourself! You do this all the time anyway, without critical thought or intentional purpose, and often without even an awareness that it is happening.

Taking thoughts captive and measuring them against God's word is a comparative process - *this is what my thought is, compared to (measured up against) what God's word says about that*. If the thought is contrary to God's word, tell yourself that it is a lie and a deception. Affirm to yourself that instead of allowing the deceptive thought to continue, you will think about, or dwell on, "Whatever is true, whatever is honorable, whatever is right, whatever is pure, whatever is lovely, whatever is of good repute, if there is any excellence... [or] anything worthy of praise" (Philippians 4:8). This spiritual battle is a daily, sometimes even hourly, discipline as you walk on the narrow way with God.

> Finally, brethren, whatever is true, whatever is honorable, whatever is right, whatever is pure, whatever is lovely, whatever is of good repute, if there is any excellence and if anything worthy of praise, dwell on these things. (Philippians 4:8)

SOBER MINDED

Ethan was thoughtful as he stared at the silver spoon he had used to stir his coffee after adding the cream which Sandra had brought back to the table. He slid his finger back and forth along the smooth handle.

"I haven't been living my faith like a warrior," he confessed to Jonathon. "My defenses against sin and Satan are not really set up. I mean, I'm very familiar with scripture after being raised in a Christian home and going to church all my life, but I can't honestly say that I have stored it up in my heart like a treasure, and that I draw upon it daily to measure and compare it with my thoughts and what the world says."

"Ethan, warriors are trained very intentionally," Jonathon emphasized. "Those skills and practices don't just happen without planning and purpose. That's why we have committed to walk this narrow way together, to learn and train from scripture, and then to encourage, strengthen, coach, and challenge one another in our faith journey."

Ethan nodded in agreement, "I have not taken seriously enough the fact that Satan wants to destroy me, my faith, and my family. I really need to become disciplined in the practice of being alert and sober-minded; and I need to discipline my eyes too. It's been easy to tell myself that as long as I don't act out in some really sinful way, there is no harm done. But it even sounds dumb just to say that out loud now."

Ethan shook his head in disbelief. He felt foolish for having been taught from the Bible all his life, but never feeling a concern that he might be targeted for destruction by Satan, even though that is what the Bible says.

"The truth is sobering, Ethan," Jonathon responded. "Remember, though, that God is walking with us each day. It says in Psalm 119:18 that it is God who opens our eyes that we may behold wonderful things from His law. I am thankful that He is opening our eyes to show and teach us these truths today, when we are ready to act on them and take responsibility for living as He designed us to live. He directs our steps each day, and He delivers us from evil. Let's bring this all to the Lord together in prayer. This is sobering and humbling stuff, but it is also exciting to see how God is leading us on the narrow way!"

The two men bowed their heads there in the restaurant booth and laid bare their souls before God and each other.

Discussion and Discipline

- Jesus said the eye is the lamp of the body, filling the body with either light or darkness. It is immensely critical what you allow into your "lamp", determining whether your eye is clear (healthy) or bad (unhealthy). On a scale of 1 to 10 (1 is the weakest to 10 being the strongest), grade the strength of your current discipline regarding the lust of the eyes? How will you commit to be more disciplined?

- How disciplined is your response in turning your eyes away when your eyes fall upon an alluring sight that triggers a lustful appetite? Is it immediate? If not, what thoughts have you told yourself to justify your continued gaze? As you take in God's word and then use it to measure and compare with your thoughts, are your thoughts true or are they lies?

- Are there any lies or deceptions which you have allowed to govern your thoughts as speculations raised up against the knowledge of God (2 Corinthians 10:5)? Describe some of those lies. Will you measure them up against the truth of God and destroy them when they are proven to be lies? Consider talking out loud about them with a trusted Christian brother.

- Have you already started a daily discipline of treasuring God's word, reading, and storing it up in your heart (Psalm 119:9-11)? If not, what will be your commitment today, and how will you begin that discipline?

- Policing your thoughts is a new discipline for many men. While Self-talk is normal and happens without exception for every man, very few consciously engage with their thoughts in a deliberate, intentional manner which is transformative, as the Bible teaches (Romans 12:1-2). What are the steps and practices you can start today, as you grow in this spiritual discipline?

Chapter Twelve

The Boastful Pride of Life

Put Aside Arrogant Assumptions

Ethan and Jonathon had attended a men's breakfast at their church, followed by working together for a couple hours of service work, helping with yard care and handyman work for some of the elderly in their congregation. Ethan enjoyed the exercise and physical work of helping in the yard, especially knowing how difficult it was for some to maintain their homes themselves. After finishing their work assignments for the morning, they stopped by the coffee shop for some cool down time, along with conversation and coffee.

"It sure felt good to be physically active this morning, after sitting at a desk all week." Ethan gave a slight groan as he sat down in the upholstered chair. "But I'm sure I'll feel the ache in every muscle in my body when I get out of bed tomorrow morning!"

"I think I'll be hearing the same complaints from my body," Jonathon agreed. "Isn't it interesting how the best things for maintaining our physical health and strength involve a feeling of suffering and discomfort? It's like that with spiritual exercise, as well; it is always uncomfortable, and could even be painful, to discipline the flesh, to take thoughts captive, or to turn your eyes away from sin and lust. But it is so good to grow stronger and consistent in those practices, knowing that each one is a denial of Self and an acknowledgment of the kingdom [reign] of God within."

Ethan nodded, and said, "Jonathon, I am becoming more and more aware of my thoughts and appetites these last few weeks; and I'm finding it is a difficult thing to change these lifelong habits. I am amazed, though, at some themes and recurring thoughts I have identified. And the unguarded thoughts seem to coordinate with lusts of the flesh without me even realizing it!

"For example, on Wednesday, I had a lousy day at work; just a lot of stuff went wrong, and I didn't get home until 8:00 pm. I had eaten nothing since lunch and I knew Alicia had a plate of food for me in the refrigerator. But I looked in the pantry and saw a package of candy bars. My mouth started watering, which is like saying my flesh lusted for that candy bar, and my thoughts said, '*Go ahead, you had such a hard, long day, and you deserve to treat yourself now with a candy bar.*' But then, from another place in my head, I heard a different voice, saying, '*A candy bar is a lousy supper, and it would be hurtful to choose that over the dinner plate Alicia set aside for you. Take that thought captive!*'"

Jonathon slapped his knee, laughed out loud, and leaned forward to give Ethan a high-five. "That's great, Ethan! Way to talk to yourself! A man's thoughts, flesh, and eyes have had a lifetime to work together in service to Self. But God and His word are powerful, working within you to transform your life, especially as you have been studying the Bible and taking it in each day. That truth is the key for measuring those speculations and lofty things raised up against the knowledge of God.

"Speaking of measuring up our thoughts, we should finish up looking at that third area of the 1 John 2:16 appetite triad, *the boastful pride of life.*"

PRIDE HAS A FEROCIOUS APPETITE

Let us remind ourselves of the stark warning Paul wrote to the church of Philippi, saying:

> Brethren, join in following my example, and observe those who walk according to the pattern you have in us. For many walk, of whom I often told you, and now tell you even weeping, that they are enemies of the cross of Christ, whose end is destruction, whose god is their appetite, and whose glory is in their shame, who set their minds on earthly things. (Philippians 3:17-19)

Those *whose god is their appetite*, who set their minds on earthly things, are enemies of the cross of Christ. The Greek word that is translated as appetite is *koilia*, which refers to the "*belly, stomach, womb, etc.; by extension: the source of feelings and emotions*" (NIV Exhaustive Concordance Dictionary. Copyright © 2015 by Zondervan). Every man has a hunger for validation and significance. That appetite is never satisfied by earthly things, but men sure try! It is ideal for these needs to be filled and satisfied throughout childhood development by parental love and support, and by encouragement and affirmation from others in positions of influence (teachers, pastors, and extended family members). Then, in adulthood, these needs are met by a spouse in the home, by good friends in the community, and by supervisors at work.

Ultimately, our significance is truly and fully realized in our relationship with God. However, if that need is not met, and especially if it is left grossly unsatisfied, a man will try to fill that empty cup himself. He often tries to meet that need by what the Bible calls the boastful pride of life. We read about it in 1 John 2.

> Do not love the world nor the things in the world. If anyone loves the world, the love of the Father is not in him. For all that is in the world, the lust of the flesh and the lust of the eyes and the boastful pride of life, is not from the Father, but is from the world. (1 John 2:15-16)

We have reviewed the first two of the three broad areas of appetite which will wreak havoc if allowed a foothold in a man's life: the lust of the flesh and the lust of the eyes. The boastful pride of life should sound familiar to us; we know that pride was the deadly spiritual venom which poisoned mankind through the devil's deception in the garden of Eden, and that it was passed to all men in their birth.

Pride is the stimulant and fuel for Self to rebel against God. The boastful pride of life spoken of here in 1 John means *arrogant assumptions, a vainglorious display*. Man is tempted to engage in this boastful pride in four areas of life: making arrogant assumptions of the future, of the past, of what he thinks of himself, and of what he thinks he knows about others.

ASSUMPTIONS ABOUT THE FUTURE

In James 4, we read an example of this evil boasting:

> Come now, you who say, "Today or tomorrow we will go to such and such a city, and spend a year there and engage in business and make a profit." Yet you do not know what your life will be like tomorrow. You are just a vapor that appears for a little while and then vanishes away. Instead, you ought to say, "If the Lord wills, we will live and also do

this or that." But as it is, you boast in your arrogance; all such boasting
is evil. Therefore, to one who knows the right thing to do and does not
do it, to him it is sin. (James 4:13-17)

James reminds the reader of their entire dependence on God by acknowledging that
a man's life is like a vapor that is short-lived and then disappears in a moment. Humility
recognizes that every breath is gifted to man by God, and that He has every right and
all power to determine when each man draws his final breath. But even the Christian
man has often been so conformed to the world and its values that his thoughts, goals,
and presumptions of power, riches, fame, and glory are touted with pomp and fanfare.
This is the hallmark of Self on display and in defiance of God.

A man conjures up dreams of grand success in future business or personal achieve-
ments and boasts of what he will accomplish. These are *arrogant assumptions*, since
finite man does not know what even the next minute will bring. This truth shines
light on the speculation that men should somehow create a vision in their mind of
what they wish to achieve, and accept nothing less than the realization of that vision.
The assumption is contrary to the prayer Jesus taught his disciples to pray in Matthew
6:9-13, that the Father would "Give us this day our daily bread."

There is certainly no evil in planning about and for the future, even as James
says to do in verse 15, "If the Lord wills, we will live and also do this or that." But
without the humble preface acknowledging entire dependence on God, it is an arrogant
assumption, the boastful pride of life that proclaims to know what will happen in the
future.

ASSUMPTIONS ABOUT PAST ACCOMPLISHMENT

It is the same arrogant assumption to boast of one's accomplishment in the past. The
assumption is that one achieved success or greatness by one's own strength, skill, effort,
or will. Arrogance does not acknowledge that God grants the life, strength, skill, and
energy for all achievement. Devoid of humility, man looks upon past actions to validate
and substantiate his value and worth within the limitations of those actions alone,
pridefully boasting of them as his accomplishments.

Jesus told a parable about such a man who had truly achieved great economic and
financial success, and warned His disciples to guard their attitudes about these matters.

And He told them a parable, saying, "The land of a rich man was very productive. And he began reasoning to himself, saying, 'What shall I do, since I have no place to store my crops?' Then he said, 'This is what I will do: I will tear down my barns and build larger ones, and there I will store all my grain and my goods. And I will say to my soul, "Soul, you have many goods laid up for many years to come; take your ease, eat, drink and be merry."' But God said to him, 'You fool! This very night your soul is required of you; and now who will own what you have prepared?' So is the man who stores up treasure for himself, and is not rich toward God." (Luke 12:16-21)

This man's arrogant assumption (boastful pride of life) was that his accomplishment had provided him security and a life of ease for many years ahead, when in fact, God was taking his soul from this world that very night. The man was a proud fool, not recognizing that his efforts and actions of the past were an enabling gift from God, or that even continued breath in his lungs would be at the discretion of God alone. The posture of humility before God would be one of thanksgiving and gratitude for great provision, and a willing heart to steward those resources for whatever length of time and in whatever manner God would determine.

ASSUMPTIONS ABOUT SELF

The boastful pride of life inclines a man to have a higher view of himself than he ought and a conversely lower view of others than he ought, and he then holds those two ill-measured views in a comparison which elevates his status. This falsely weighted comparison with others happens constantly within the heart of man, and often without conscious or intentional thought. Whether walking into a restaurant, a neighbor's home, the work office, or a Sunday morning worship service, this unrestrained appetite of boastful pride will always provide a man with a distorted view of himself compared to others.

Jesus was at a dinner gathering when He admonished his fellow guests about this tendency to elevate oneself compared to others, recorded in Luke 14.

And He began speaking a parable to the invited guests when He noticed how they had been picking out the places of honor at the table,
saying to them, "When you are invited by someone to a wedding feast,
do not take the place of honor, for someone more distinguished than
you may have been invited by him, and he who invited you both will
come and say to you, 'Give your place to this man,' and then in disgrace
you proceed to occupy the last place. But when you are invited, go
and recline at the last place, so that when the one who has invited you
comes, he may say to you, 'Friend, move up higher'; then you will have
honor in the sight of all who are at the table with you. For everyone
who exalts himself will be humbled, and he who humbles himself will
be exalted." (Luke 14:7-11)

The problem causing a man's tendency to overestimate his own status when compared to others is that we do not ever see ourselves very well. Paul describes this truth
in 1 Corinthians 13:12, where he writes, "For now we see in a mirror dimly." Who are
you looking at in a mirror? Yourself, of course! The Greek word translated as dimly in
this verse literally means, *in a riddle,* as if it is difficult or impossible for a man to see
himself or figure himself out. Jesus told a second parable illustrating this issue in Luke
18 about a Pharisee and a tax collector.

And He also told this parable to some people who trusted in themselves
that they were righteous, and viewed others with contempt: "Two men
went up into the temple to pray, one a Pharisee and the other a tax
collector. The Pharisee stood and was praying this to himself: 'God, I
thank You that I am not like other people: swindlers, unjust, adulterers,
or even like this tax collector. I fast twice a week; I pay tithes of all
that I get.' But the tax collector, standing some distance away, was even
unwilling to lift up his eyes to heaven, but was beating his breast, saying,
'God, be merciful to me, the sinner!' I tell you, this man went to his
house justified rather than the other; for everyone who exalts himself
will be humbled, but he who humbles himself will be exalted." (Luke
18:9-14)

ASSUMPTIONS ABOUT OTHERS

A man's arrogant assumptions (boastful pride of life) about others will interfere with or damage his relationships with other people. Arrogant assumptions about others include the belief that one knows what others are thinking, or what their motivations are, or what they have done to you or said about you. This is with no clear evidence to know if such things are true. Almost every one of us can honestly recall an occasion, when in a heated argument (usually with someone we care about deeply), we have said to the other one, "*I know exactly what you are thinking!*" That statement is always false. It is the boastful pride of life agitating and fueling Self; all kinds of sin and hurtful things will follow if it is not nipped in the bud. The same is true of being certain you know what another person's motives are when they have not said anything to validate your belief.

Paul writes about this in 1 Corinthians 2:11: "For who among men knows the thoughts of a man except the spirit of the man which is in him? Even so the thoughts of God no one knows except the Spirit of God." A humble disposition toward others recognizes that we cannot know or assume the thoughts or motivations of another person.

SOBER-MINDED

Jonathon set his empty coffee cup down on the side table next to his chair and leaned forward. "Ethan, I want to tell you about a time I struggled with this boastful pride of life. It will be good for me to share this with you. I told you how your dad and I partnered up and walked this narrow way together the last twenty years of his life. Also, how after Conner was born, he talked with me about wanting to come alongside you as a new father and walk together in the same way. I remember it was the week after Conner was born that your dad and I met to walk a trail in the state park. As we walked, he was so excited to tell me about his plans to connect with you regularly, and to build a partnership of faith with you.

"All I could think about was that he was getting ready to tell me he wouldn't have the time to continue meeting with me each week, that it was time for me to find another partner. Ethan, he never said that, or gave any sign he was thinking or feeling that. But for about three months, I allowed myself to believe that the next time we met he would finally tell me. I felt like I was dying inside, Ethan; I was grieving the end of a wonderful friendship that wasn't even close to ending! It was all because I believed I knew what he was thinking, and that lie messed with my thoughts in so many awful ways. Finally, your dad asked me what was going on with me. He asked how he could help me, because he realized I was struggling with something.

"You could have knocked him over with your little finger when I told him what I thought was going to happen – that I felt I knew what he was thinking. He was shocked! Then he wept; he was so sad that I believed he would abandon our friendship. As I look back on that time, I can't even imagine how I let myself be convinced by the arrogant assumption that I knew what he was thinking. But I know that Satan is on the prowl, always looking for vulnerabilities that he can exploit. That's why we must be diligent in reading scripture, being alert and sober-minded, and praying at all times."

"Jonathon, that had to be an awful time for you," Ethan said. "And I am under-standing how devastating it could be to lose that, even though we've only been on this narrow way together for several months. I have never thought about how hard it must have been for you when dad died so unexpectedly, and you really lost that friendship. I'm sorry, Jonathon."

Jonathon smiled as he thoughtfully responded, "Thank you, Ethan. Yes, it was hard. But not in the same way as when I was believing the lie. When God decided your dad was drawing his final breath, and then took him home to His presence, it was very sad and yet joyful at the same time. I knew we had walked the narrow way together right up to the entrance of heaven for him. I trust God with that decision of when there will be no more tomorrows for us on this earth. And now, I am overjoyed that I can walk this same narrow way with you. Because of that, I am a much richer man than I ever thought I could be."

Discussion and Discipline

- The boastful pride of life is a complex phrase to wrap your head around. Knowing that the literal translation is arrogant assumptions, does it make it easier to identify when you experience this prideful appetite? When you identify it within you, do you take steps to choose humility, that place of entire dependence on God? How difficult is that for you?

- Taking a posture of humility toward others, and inviting them to have the best seats, park in the closest parking spaces, and get in line ahead of you would be a dramatic change of demeanor for most of us. Does it seem possible to consistently hold this view toward others? What would get in the way of that happening? What are some ways you can think of to immediately begin this discipline of practice?

- Have you imagined that you know what someone else is thinking, or have you made the arrogant assumption that you know what their motivations are? What would be the best practice to stop engaging in these prideful assumptions?

- Do you plan for the future being humbly mindful that it is entirely in the hands of God, or have you had the tendency to proclaim what will happen in the future, as if it is something under your control? When things don't turn out as you had planned, are you able to release it into God's hands?

- The boastful pride of life regarding past accomplishments likes to compare to, and "one-up", others. When you are in conversation with others, is it tempting to always tell a better story, or explain how you were more successful than they expressed with their experience? How might it affect those relationships if you let their story be the best one, and expressed great interest in learning more about them?

AREAS OF STEWARDSHIP

The Disciplines of Spiritual Formation in Five
Areas of Stewardship

DDS

DDS Publishing

Chapter Thirteen

Personal Stewardship

You are God's Steward

Ethan and Jonathon were enjoying a morning hike on a state park trail. This trail was a comfortable hike, both in difficulty and length, as it wound its way through the pine trees that surrounded a beautiful lake nestled in a valley at the base of mountains on three sides. It was a great opportunity for the men to walk and talk, and to pray, while appreciating the magnitude of God's creation. Ethan found it to be the perfect setting to pose a question he had been considering for a long time; he wanted to know if Jonathon had thought about and wrestled with the same idea.

"Jonathon," Ethan said, "Over these last months, we've studied scripture together and talked about a lot of really important spiritual concepts and real-life issues. After we agreed to partner up to walk the narrow way together, we first worked through these foundations of truth in the Bible: how God created us, how sin first entered man and the world, the ongoing consequences of sin, redemption through Christ, and the establishment of the kingdom of God within the hearts of men. Then we focused on spiritual battles: our struggles with the world, the flesh, and the devil, the daily practices of denying Self, and controlling appetites as we take up our cross and follow Jesus. Many of those conversations were had "as needed" to address the genuine struggles I was having at the time!

"I have learned so much and found joy and strength in this daily walk with you and God. Conner is almost five years old now, and I have been thinking about the next ten to twelve years. I want to train and prepare him as well as I can to walk the narrow way, and I wish I had a map to follow in that instruction, or an outline of the disciplines and practices to be mindful of as I teach him. I would love to help him build a life that is already shaped and disciplined for walking humbly with God. Does that make sense?"

"It sure does make sense!" Jonathon agreed. "That same map, or outline, is what we should follow as adult men, as well. Your dad and I actually talked at length about this idea for many years, and tried hard to apply it and hold each other accountable to those disciplines. I think it's exciting that you have been thinking along these same lines, and it's especially great that you are contemplating how you will train and instruct Conner as he grows!

"Everything flows from being in right relationship with God, humbly walking with Him in that place of entire dependence on Him. This is the most fundamental and foundational truth; if you miss that, everything else about your spiritual view will be distorted and cockeyed. As we walk humbly with God, the understanding of our spiritual reality and the life we live each day is anchored to the foundations of truth found in scripture. These foundations are critical to understand because they bring clarity to our perspective and guide our approach to addressing everything else we experience and respond to, like the daily battles we fight.

The last portion of that map I would call the disciplines of spiritual formation. They will shape, hone, and focus our perspective and the practice of our humble posture toward God. We always recognize that we are His creation, and life and breath are given to us by Him. We are simply stewards of this life and the resources He entrusts to us.

I would categorize these disciplines into five domains of stewardship: Personal, Household, "One Another" (the church), Vocation, and Community."

"This sounds really outstanding! I would love to understand those," Ethan said. "Could we get started today?"

"You bet!" Jonathon agreed. "You've really started and even developed many of these disciplines, Ethan. But it is a helpful thing to see the big picture, and how there is a unity of truth, with all the elements related to each other, especially as a father teaching his son."

They came to a clearing along the shoreline with some benches and picnic tables, and Jonathon motioned for Ethan to follow him to a bench, where he plopped down, saying, "I'm ready to give my old legs a break. Let's rest here for a while and dig into the disciplines of personal stewardship. We'll see that this discipline includes worship, understanding your gifts and skills, and living with integrity."

LOVE IS FIRST—THE FOUNDATION OF ALL CHRISTIAN DISCIPLINES

As we look into the disciplines within this domain of stewardship, we must always be mindful that all true Christian disciplines grow and develop from, and are motivated by, love for God and love for others. In Mark 12, a scribe asked Jesus which commandment is the foremost, and He answers, saying,

> "The foremost [commandment] is, 'Hear, O Israel! The Lord our God is one Lord; and you shall love the Lord your God with all your heart, and with all your soul, and with all your mind, and with all your strength.' The second is this, 'You shall love your neighbor as yourself.' There is no other commandment greater than these." (Mark 12:29-31)

Review 1 Corinthians 13 to understand how otherwise good spiritual activities and characteristics are utterly meaningless and without value if love is absent. This chapter also paints a portrait of love and its attributes:

> Love is patient, love is kind and is not jealous; love does not brag and is not arrogant, does not act unbecomingly; it does not seek its own, is not provoked, does not take into account a wrong suffered, does not rejoice in unrighteousness, but rejoices with the truth; bears all things, believes all things, hopes all things, endures all things. (1 Corinthians 13:4–7)

Being created in the image of God, relationships with others are at the center of a man's purposeful and meaningful engagement with the world around him. This is evidenced by Jesus' declaration that the "foremost" and the second greatest commandments are to love the Lord your God with all your heart, soul, mind, and strength, and to love your neighbor as yourself.

Personal stewardship is the intentional and responsible management and care of a man for his own spiritual development and his daily walk in relationship with God.

It includes ensuring that one's behavior and practices are in alignment, or are coming into alignment, with the truth of God's word. When there is integrity between God's word and our practices, we bring honor and praise to the Lord.

WORSHIP

The Attitude of Worship – Walking Humbly With God

This is a life of worship, and true worship begins and ends with humility; being in right relationship with God. That is, recognizing and acknowledging the truth that above and before all other things, we are God's creation. He is God, and we exist in a place of entire dependence on God. He is the source of every breath we draw, and the stimulus for every beat of our heart.

Understanding and recognizing this truth is humility, and God requires that we walk humbly with Him (Micah 6:8). Jesus described the forthcoming nature of true worship by true worshipers in John 4 saying:

> "But an hour is coming, and now is, when the true worshipers will worship the Father in spirit and truth; for such people the Father seeks to be His worshipers. God is spirit, and those who worship Him must worship in spirit and truth." (John 4:23-24)

True Worshipers are those who are restored to right relationship with God, and who humbly bow low in their spirit in adoration of the Father. Worshiping in *spirit* and *truth* refers to the inner man or spirit of the man (as opposed to the mind or soul with its emotions, or the physical body with its movement and actions). It also refers to integrity, or the state of being genuine, as demonstrated by facts, and being obedient in behavior and practice.

There are routine and regular times of worship expression which include songs of praise and confession of God's glory and magnificence. There are also moments of unscripted and ecstatic worship as God's grace, mercy, and kindness break through the trials of daily life and are recognized with joy. Worship is expressed in our times of contrition, sorrow, and lament as we offer our lives in each moment of every type to our Lord as living sacrifices. There is not a prescribed location for worship or a correct style of worship.

Acts of Worship

Pray without ceasing

The posture of humility, the place of entire dependence on God, will create within us an ever-deepening yearning to hear His voice and be taught by His Spirit. Paul reflects on this in 1 Thessalonians 5:16-18, writing, "Rejoice always; pray without ceasing; in everything give thanks; for this is God's will for you in Christ Jesus."

You may wonder what it looks like to pray without ceasing. Remember that you are walking humbly with God always. After Jesus ascended to heaven forty days following His resurrection, the Father sent the Holy Spirit to be *with* and to be *in* Christians forever, and to teach them all things (John 14:16-17, 26). If we are spending a day with a person who is important to us (spouse, best friend, parent, or child), we are in a stream of unending communication with them as we walk together, encountering and sharing in the events and moments of the day. We interact with each other as we observe and respond to the ebb and flow of that day's life. In this way, we walk humbly together with God throughout each day. As you walk out to your mailbox, you notice your neighbor who kicks at his lawnmower that won't start. You share your observation with God, praying, *Lord; he looks so angry. Please encourage him and give him the strength and wisdom he needs for today.* God may respond with the suggestion that you are the one to walk over right now, and share that encouraging word, help, and wisdom with your neighbor!

> Rejoice always; pray without ceasing; in everything give thanks; for this is God's will for you in Christ Jesus. (1 Thessalonians 5:16-17)

> Be devoted to one another in brotherly love; give preference to one another in honor; not lagging behind in diligence, fervent in spirit,

serving the Lord; rejoicing in hope, persevering in tribulation, devoted to prayer. (Romans 12:10–12)

But you, when you pray, go into your inner room, close your door and pray to your Father who is in secret, and your Father who sees what is done in secret will reward you. (Matthew 6:6)

We are God's stewards. He is in us and walks with us at all times, and from that relationship, we share with Him our responses to the events and thoughts of the day. We talk, we listen, we respond, and we act in this very personal continuous relationship with our Lord.

Reading the Bible

Reading the Bible is an essential daily practice for the Christian man. The Bible is the written, inerrant word of God. It is the truth through which He reveals Himself, His attributes, His character, and His principles. We learn from God's word the truth of man's creation and his right and natural relationship to God, his Creator. We also learn of the fall of man from that relationship, and the lengths to which God went to provide the narrow way of redemption from sin and death through His Son, Jesus Christ.

God's word, the scripture, shines the light of truth on the distortions, lies, and deceptions of the world. As we read the Bible daily, the Holy Spirit teaches us and explains what we are reading and learning. In Psalm 119:18, the psalmist prays that God will "Open my eyes, that I may behold wonderful things from Your law." As Jesus said, this is the role of the Holy Spirit, who teaches us and opens our eyes to understand the truths in scripture.

This process of reading and studying God's word daily is an act of worship, acknowledging our need to know and understand God's truth, and in that process, to be transformed by the renewing of our mind (Romans 12:1-2).

Giving to God and Others

Some would say that the best way for others to identify what you worship is by watching to see what you pay closest attention to, what captures your interest, and that to which you are continuously looking. What is the focus of your heart? Jesus confirms this perspective in Matthew 6, when He explains that if you watch to see where people store up their treasure, you will know where their heart is focused:

> "Do not store up for yourselves treasures on earth, where moth and rust destroy, and where thieves break in and steal. But store up for yourselves treasures in heaven, where neither moth nor rust destroys, and where thieves do not break in or steal; for where your treasure is, there your heart will be also." (Matthew 6:19-21)

> "No one can serve two masters; for either he will hate the one and love the other, or he will be devoted to one and despise the other. You cannot serve God and wealth." (Matthew 6:24)

Everything on the earth is God's, and He distributes resources to whom He wishes (Psalm 24:1). Holding the money He has given you with open hands, asking God for His instruction on how to use, apply, or give your money is an act of worship. That is why, in the same statement, Jesus spoke of your heart being located where you store your treasure, and that no one can serve two masters. The Bible instructs us in Colossians 3 that "Whatever you do in word or deed, do all in the name of the Lord Jesus, giving thanks through Him to God the Father" (Colossians 3:17).

"*Whatever*" certainly includes how we handle our money, so the manner in which we spend and share His money is fundamentally an act of worship. Christians are instructed to set aside money weekly to give to support the ministry of the gospel (1 Corinthians 16:1-2). Jesus also said that the manner in which we share our resources (money, food, clothing, care) with others is an act of worship, of relating to Him. He says in Matthew 25, "To the extent that you did it to one of these brothers of Mine, even the least of them, you did it to Me" (Matthew 25:34-40).

Denying Self

The daily action of denying Self, taking up our cross, and following Jesus is an act of worship (Luke 9:23). Jesus speaks about the obvious when He said, "No one can serve two masters; for either he will hate the one and love the other, or he will be devoted to one and despise the other" (Matthew 6:24). Every decision to deny Self is an act of worship to our Lord, acknowledging and being obedient to our one and only Master.

TALENTS AND ABILITIES

Identify Your Talents and Abilities

God created every man with innate interests, skills, and abilities. These inherent characteristics are often determined or influenced by genetics, environment, and practice. A basketball player may be an example of this. Because he is tall and coordinated (genetics), he has an advantage over others under the basket. In addition, if he diligently rehearses (practice, or training) the various skills of basketball, his play may rise to a level of excellence which someone who is short and lacking in coordination would never hope to achieve.

Those things which interest us the most are often a reflection of abilities and skills for which we have the potential to cultivate and develop. As a boy grows into a young man, he is limited in the knowledge of his own natural talent and the potential for skills development because of lack of exposure to a variety of tasks. He has had no opportunity to discover many areas that he might be interested in pursuing. So, a young man should attempt many things!

He will discover or confirm if he is interested in working with mechanical things, or with technology, or with numbers and accounting, or with language and speaking or teaching. Interest or curiosity are key factors in a person's willingness to take the risk of trying something new. Sadly, many people feel so paralyzed by the fear of failure or looking foolish that they are unwilling to even try something new to them. This is because the cruel voice of Self wants to protect one's image, and discourages taking any risk or exploring things that are unknown to us. If a toddler refused to take a step until he knew he would never fall, he would never learn to walk!

We learn and grow, learn and grow. The stairway to success in any new endeavor includes multiple treads of trial and error; each failure is the riser to a new and necessary tread to the top. We can trust God with every step we take, knowing He is always with us and directing those steps. God has equipped each man for the life which He has prepared for him, and He will certainly provide the opportunity to discover and cultivate those interests.

Practice and Cultivate Your Talents and Abilities

Once interests and abilities are discovered, it is necessary and responsible to practice and develop the skills to perform those tasks well. A newborn baby is not very good at doing anything. Skills like crawling, walking, talking, jumping, and running are slowly learned, practiced, and then developed to great proficiency.

The same is true in later stages of development concerning helpful and employable skills and tasks. Care and diligence must be taken to practice them over and over, to hone skills and increase their validity and value. This is very important for implementing your talents and skills, whether in your vocation, caring for your household, or helping others. This will also affect all the other disciplines of stewardship.

Share Your Talents and Abilities

In Hebrews 13:16, we read this instruction: "And do not neglect doing good and sharing, for with such sacrifices God is pleased." Because we excel in a practice, it's easy to take for granted our talents and skills, thinking that they are not so significant or of great value. But to others who are not so capable in that practice, having a great need can be overwhelming and discouraging. When you do good and share your talents in serving others, they are blessed, and God is pleased!

Jesus tells us in Matthew 5:14-16, "You are the light of the world... Let your light shine before men in such a way that they may see your good works, and glorify your Father who is in heaven." Applying our talents and abilities in such a way (good works) that others are encouraged and helped, glorifies our heavenly Father. It is also a demonstration of obedience to Jesus' new commandment in the Gospel of John.

> "A new commandment I give to you, that you love one another, even as I have loved you, that you also love one another. By this all men will know that you are My disciples, if you have love for one another." (John 13:34-35)

We are to love one another with our words, our care and support, and with our talents and abilities. In this way, all men will know that we are Jesus' disciples!

SPIRITUAL GIFTS

Identify Your Spiritual Gifts

While God endows every person with innate talents and abilities, spiritual gifts are very different. Spiritual gifts are not related to or connected with genetics or innate abilities. They are given through the Holy Spirit only to those who have placed their faith in Jesus Christ for their salvation. The man who becomes a Christian often discovers, through his relationship with other Christians, that others can identify a spiritual gift operating in his life, even if he is not yet aware of this gift.

There is a good reason for this to be the case. The Holy Spirit gives spiritual gifts to each one in the church to build up and strengthen the body of Christ. Spiritual gifts are never for one's own benefit, or to elevate our social standing or position. They are always meant for the service of others.

There are three explicit references to spiritual gifts in the Bible; they are Romans 12, 1 Corinthians 12, and Ephesians 4. We see a variety of gifts listed (it is not indicated whether these are limited or exhaustive lists). In Romans 12, the listed spiritual gifts are: prophesy, serving, teaching, exhortation, generosity, leading, and mercy (Romans 12:3-8). We find that in 1 Corinthians 12, the list includes wisdom, knowledge, faith, healing, miracles, prophesy, discernment of spirits, tongues, interpretation of tongues, helps, and administrations (1 Corinthians 12:4-11, 28-31). Finally, in Ephesians 4, the gifts of apostles, prophets, evangelists, and pastors and teachers are given to the church "for the equipping of the saints for the work of service, to the building up of the body of Christ; until we all attain to the unity of the faith, and of the knowledge of the Son of God, to a mature man, to the measure of the stature which belongs to the fullness of Christ" (Ephesians 4:11-13). The second half of 1 Corinthians 12 emphasizes how the uniqueness of how God created and bestows gifts to each Christian serves to benefit the whole body of Christ, just as a physical body benefits from the unique service of an arm, a foot, an eye, or an ear.

In 1 Corinthians 12, the apostle Paul writes at length to the church at Corinth regarding spiritual gifts. In verses 4-6 of this chapter, he acknowledges the varieties of gifts, ministries, and effects within the church, while it is the same God who is working all things in all persons. He completes his thought about these gifts, ministries, and effects in verse 7 by stating that "to each one is given the manifestation of the Spirit for the common good." The Greek word translated as manifestation is *"phanerōsis"*. This word is the subject of the sentence (the spiritual gift, ministry, or effect) and declares that it is *"shining"*, *"publicly shown"*, *rendered apparent"*, *"openly evident"*, an *"expression"* or *"bestowment"*.

The spiritual gift which is given to each man through the Holy Spirit is *publicly shown*, or *openly evident* for the common good or benefit of the church. This explains why others may identify a man's spiritual gift before he is even aware of it. The *expression* of a spiritual gift (which is openly evident to others) is a *manifestation* of the Holy Spirit – not of the will or fortitude of the man.

In this same chapter (12) of 1 Corinthians, verses 8-10 describe how different people are bestowed with different spiritual gifts (varieties), while verse 11 states clearly that, "<u>one and the same Spirit works all these things</u>, distributing to each one individually just as He wills." It is the Holy Spirit that is working these spiritual gifts, and He decides upon the gifts and distributes them to each individual.

Practice and Cultivate Your Spiritual Gifts

Tending to spiritual gifts differs greatly from practicing natural talents and abilities. We cannot make more of, or improve upon how the Holy Spirit is "working all these things!" On the other hand, we certainly can address the things in our life which get in the way of the effective use of our spiritual gifts to serve others. Our effective use of spiritual gifts can be inhibited or overshadowed by a life that is conformed to the world, and by relationship practices which are "Self-centered" instead of being centered on loving God and loving others. Our study of, and devotion to scripture is essential for our transformation by the renewing of our minds (Romans 12:2). It would be accurate to say that we need to get our Self out of the way, and welcome the Holy Spirit's lead and direction in our relationships and activities.

The daily denial of Self and taking up our cross is fundamental to this work of the Holy Spirit in our lives. Paul writes to Timothy to be "constantly nourished on the words of the faith and of the sound doctrine which you have been following", and to "discipline yourself for the purpose of godliness" (1 Timothy 4:6-8). The effective manifestation of the Holy Spirit through spiritual gifts will always be centered on building up others in the body of Christ, with the goal of attaining unity of faith and knowledge of the Son of God.

Share your Spiritual Gifts

Finally, we read in 1 Peter 4:10, "As each one has received a special gift, employ it in serving one another as good stewards of the manifold grace of God." As we explore all areas of stewardship, we will see how our spiritual gifts matter, and are important in our relationships with others in the church, and in our community. When we humbly engage the gifts which God has given us for the service and love of others, it is an act of personal stewardship as God's creation. This glorifies God and lifts up the name of Jesus!

INTEGRITY

Alignment of Values and Behavior

The Bible addresses and condemns hypocrisy at length, and Jesus was consistent in speaking harshly about the hypocrisy of the scribes and Pharisees. Hypocrisy is when a person claims to believe a certain way but then acts differently; there is not an alignment between what he says and his behavior. In Matthew 23, Jesus draws a morbid picture of hypocrites, saying,

"Woe to you, scribes and Pharisees, hypocrites! For you are like white-washed tombs which on the outside appear beautiful, but inside they are full of dead men's bones and all uncleanness. So you, too, outwardly appear righteous to men, but inwardly you are full of hypocrisy and lawlessness." (Matthew 23:27-28)

Integrity is lost, and a hypocrite is born when a man speaks words in such a way because he wants others to credit him with righteousness, but he is not willing to take the actions that align with those words. It is evident his words are evil and deceitful, contrary to scripture's admonition in 1 Peter 3:10, which says, "The one who desires life, to love and see good days, must keep his tongue from evil and his lips from speaking deceit." The discipline of integrity to which we must attend is a threshold over which many stumble and cannot bring themselves to cross. But it is where faith merges with behavior and becomes evidence of the transformed life.

Decision-making

A wise approach to making decisions that are guided by scripture and formed through prayer is evidence of a life spent humbly walking with God. The making of a decision is straightforward if scripture prohibits an action, such as theft. In Exodus 20:15, God commands that you shall not steal. It is also simple when scripture directs you to take action, like Romans 13:7 instructing you to pay your taxes. In other decisions, the whole counsel of scripture should be considered. Think about how the decision may affect other people or other areas of stewardship. Scripture also highlights the value of getting wise counsel from others with more experience and wisdom (Proverbs 11:14, 12:15, 15:22).

Perseverance

There are several meaningful words that are rightly associated with perseverance: resilience, persistence, and steadfastness. All these words are characteristic of the discipline of personal stewardship through times of difficulty, sorrow, trouble, or hardship. They describe the Christian man who presses forward even when unexpected difficulties thwart progress, who readily adapts to stressful situations or tragedy, and who stands firm to withstand life's storms. These tumultuous situations are all encountered along the narrow way, and the man who humbly walks with God is not detoured as he struggles forward. Romans 5 describes the growth and maturity which develops in a man as he perseveres through trouble and tribulation, noting that tribulation brings about perseverance; and perseverance, proven character.

> And not only this, but we also exult in our tribulations, knowing that tribulation brings about perseverance; and perseverance, proven character; and proven character, hope; and hope does not disappoint, because the love of God has been poured out within our hearts through the Holy Spirit who was given to us. (Romans 5:3-5)

The duplicity of Self is revealing, in that Self tries to avoid difficulty and tribulation because of the discomfort involved. Tribulation is necessary for the formation of perseverance and character in the man of God!

Dependability

Dependability and reliability have everything to do with the integrity and alignment between your words and your actions. If you make a commitment, it is essential that you follow through with performing that to which you commit.

That is dependability, when others can *depend* on you doing what you said you would do. When asked by others to engage in a commitment, it is better to say 'no' than to say 'yes' and then not follow through with corresponding action. Ecclesiastes warns us to guard our speech to ensure we are prepared to act in accordance with what we say: "It is better that you should not vow than that you should vow and not pay. Do not let your speech cause you to sin and do not say in the presence of the messenger of God that it was a mistake" (Ecclesiastes 5:5-6).

When one decides to say *yes* or *no* to a request, it is wise to leave it at that. Don't add a lot of other talking and explanations to your answer. Jesus said that an oath, or a commitment, should either be "'Yes, yes' or 'No, no'; anything beyond these is of evil."

> "Again, you have heard that the ancients were told, 'You shall not make false vows, but shall fulfill your vows to the Lord.' But I say to you,

make no oath at all, either by heaven, for it is the throne of God, or by the earth, for it is the footstool of His feet, or by Jerusalem, for it is the city of the great King. Nor shall you make an oath by your head, for you cannot make one hair white or black. But let your statement be, 'Yes, yes' or 'No, no'; anything beyond these is of evil." (Matthew 5:33-37)

UNDER CONSTRUCTION (BEING TRANSFORMED!)

Ethan looked over the notes he had been taking through their search of the scriptures and the discussion on personal stewardship. He noticed that much of his life and practice lined up with many of the things which he and Jonathon had discussed, but he also saw that there were some practices in which he was inconsistent.

He looked up at Jonathon. "What jumps out at me is integrity. Sometimes I waffle when people ask me to help with projects or with serving at church. I've got lots of excuses or reasons I can't help, but I don't just say *no*. I suppose that might sometimes be because I know I should say *yes*, so I list all the reasons I am saying *no*. But even if I must say *no*, I still do the same thing. I think it might be because I don't want people to think poorly of me."

Jonathon nodded sympathetically. "Remember that Self is always wanting to protect your reputation, and we like to think more highly of ourselves than we ought. That might cross over into acts of worship and, specifically, of denying Self. There is another consideration as you contemplate making a commitment to help others with projects and service. It is important to assess the time and energy which the commitment will require from you. It is wise to count the cost of the decision before you make it. There is so much more to be studied and learned about personal stewardship, and I'm thankful our heavenly Father sent the Holy Spirit to live with and in us, and that He is with us specifically to teach us all things" (John 14:26)!

Discussion and Discipline

- A life of worship is a life of continually recognizing and acknowledging the truth that, above and before all other things, we are God's creation. He is God, and we exist in a place of entire dependence on Him. He is the source of every breath we draw, and the stimulus for every beat of our heart. How is this view of worship different from how many Christians may see worship? How is this different from how you have viewed worship?

- Through a process of experience and opportunity, we begin to identify and practice our talents and abilities. Have you discovered and identified those areas or tasks in which you are interested, and at which you have become, or will become, more skilled as you practice them? We are admonished in Hebrews 13:16 not to "neglect doing good and sharing." Have you found regular opportunities to do good by sharing your talents with others? Think of some examples.

- Do you have relationships with other Christians for mutual encouragement and spiritual growth? Do you know the spiritual gift(s) which the Holy Spirit has bestowed upon you? Have others in the church identified that gift in you? What is it? Have you identified a spiritual gift openly evident in another Christian man's life? Talk with others about the spiritual gifts, and how they are distributed to each one individually as the Holy Spirit wills. Discuss how that parallels the unique abilities of members of a physical body, and how those members serve and support one another (1Corinthians 12:18-21).

- Building your integrity is a serious endeavor which many men do not address intentionally. Scripture clearly says that God requires integrity in the life of a man. In what ways do you see a need to pay attention to your words, practice, or behavior to strengthen your integrity? Have you identified any serious deficits in your integrity? Talk with someone you trust about this concern, and make a plan to construct this area of integrity in your life.

Chapter Fourteen

Household Stewardship

Providing, Protecting, and Planning for Your Household

Ethan and Jonathon were sitting in the upper row in a section of bleachers at the neighborhood park, discussing the narrow way while watching Connor practice tee ball. This was Connor's first experience in organized play, along with most of the other 4-year-olds. It was a great time celebrating the rare solid hit, clumsy attempts at catching and then chasing the ball, and abundant distractions like collecting rocks, pulling up grass, and just sitting down in the middle of a play because they were tired.

"I suppose watching the kids learn and attempt to practice tee ball might be like what God sees as He watches us learn about and start trying to practice new disciplines of faith," Jonathon chuckled. "We can be serious in our efforts and commitment, but new things and new thinking are always awkward and clumsy for us; sometimes we forget that something now matters to us and we slide right back into the well-worn wagon ruts of our past practices."

"Oh man, that is so true - clumsy is the right word," Ethan agreed. "I'm sure glad to know that God is patient with my efforts! Sometimes it feels like I'm trying to do things with my left hand for the first time when I'm right-handed. Things can be so simple and easy to say, but turning them into a practice is another story. Some days, I get frustrated or just plain tired out."

"I understand, Ethan," Jonathon looked over at him with genuine sympathy. "I'm convinced that is why it is so important for men to partner up for this walk on the narrow way. It can be difficult, and we need encouragement and reminders of the truth so the deceptions of the enemy don't catch us unawares. Consider also that it is less difficult if we have learned the truth as a child, and then are doing the hard work of applying that truth in practice as we grow to adulthood. It's wonderful not to have to unlearn poor practices! That's what your hope is for Connor, right? You want him to hear you teach him with the help of the Holy Spirit and then watch you practice the things you are teaching him. I'm convinced that the most impactful part for him will be watching you, and then learning by imitating your practice. An important part of a man's stewardship of his household is providing wisdom and instruction for his children, and guiding them by teaching from God's word.

"Let's look at scripture today, and see how we are to steward our household. The domain of household stewardship includes disciplines of providing, protecting, and planning for your family and home."

AS ALWAYS, LOVE IS FIRST

> Jesus answered, "The foremost [commandment] is, 'Hear, O Israel! The Lord our God is one Lord; and you shall love the Lord your God with all your heart, and with all your soul, and with all your mind, and with all your strength.' The second is this, 'You shall love your neighbor as yourself.' There is no other commandment greater than these." (Mark 12:29-31)

Being created in the image of God, relationships are at the center of a man's purposeful and meaningful engagement with the world around him. Household stewardship is the intentional and responsible management, care, and protection of one's household and family, his wife, children, and others.

PROVIDING FOR YOUR FAMILY AND HOME

Your Love and Care

Scripture instructs a man to provide love and care for his family. This includes tending to the relational needs of his household, understanding that God created them in His image. This means that healthy, supportive, and strong relationships are essential to their well-being. Paul wrote to the church in Ephesus that husbands are to love their wives sacrificially, following the example of Christ loving the church:

> Husbands, love your wives, just as Christ also loved the church and gave Himself up for her, so that He might sanctify her, having cleansed her by the washing of water with the word, that He might present to Himself the church in all her glory, having no spot or wrinkle or any such thing; but that she would be holy and blameless. So husbands ought also to love their own wives as their own bodies. He who loves his own wife loves himself; for no one ever hated his own flesh, but nourishes and cherishes it, just as Christ also does the church, because we are members of His body. (Ephesians 5:25-30)

This commitment of love and care for your wife, and a husband's daily decisions to give himself up for his wife, are a true testimony of denying Self and following Jesus.

Providing love and care for your children is grounded in understanding their vulnerability and need for compassion, training, instruction, and discipline. Psalm 103 draws a parallel between a father's compassion for his children and the Lord's compassion to those who fear Him: "Just as a father has compassion on his children, so the Lord has compassion on those who fear Him" (Psalm 103:13). It is noteworthy that the word compassion describes a father's love for his children in scripture. *Compassion is, "sympathetic consciousness of others' distress together with a desire to alleviate it" (Compassion. (2024). In Merriam-Webster Dictionary. https://www.merriam-webster .com/dictionary/compassion#dictionary-entry-1).*

A father is to always see his child's great need to be taught and trained, and to be prepared for the difficulties and rigors of life. Being moved by his compassion, a father comes alongside his children and, through relationship, he expresses his love and compassion for them as he daily addresses what they need to grow to full stature in life. Sometimes what his child needs is compassion that is gentle and tender, and other times, it is necessary for a father to be firm and stern. But always the motivation behind the expression is to be one of compassion, chosen to meet the need of his child at that moment.

In scripture, the love and compassion of a father for his child is paired multiple times with discipline and correction, as illustrated in Proverbs 3:12 and Proverbs 13:24.

For whom the Lord loves He reproves, even as a father corrects the son in whom he delights. (Proverbs 3:12)

He who withholds his rod hates his son, but he who loves him disciplines him diligently. (Proverbs 13:24)

Your Work

A man provides financially for his family and home through his work, whether it is by employment with another or by operating a business, where he is employed by all his customers. Engagement in daily work is a stewardship which was designated by God for man from the time of creation. God planted the garden of Eden and placed the man there to "cultivate it and keep it" (Genesis 2:8, 15). There was no paycheck or benefits involved. It was God's design for His creation (man) to be the steward of the resources which God entrusted to him.

Scripture is clear that God's design remains true, and it is through employment or business that a man stewards his household by providing for their financial needs. In 1 Timothy, Paul was crystal clear on this matter when he gave this admonition and warning: "But if anyone does not provide for his own, and especially for those of his household, he has denied the faith and is worse than an unbeliever" (1 Timothy 5:8).

Your response-ability

A man provides dynamic structure, order, and consistency for his family and home through his vigilant management and response-ability for his household. This play on words is intended to bring a tension to the good but overused and under-comprehended word, *responsible*. To be response-able is not only a state of being able to respond, but in addition is the readiness and willingness to take action according to the need of the moment. A Christian man is to be engaged and tuned in to the atmosphere and environment of his family and home, prepared to take action to address the needs of broken appliances, or worn-out items that need to be repaired or replaced. Family members who are hurting need comfort or encouragement, or children who are unruly need correction or discipline. When he sees those needs, he is ready and willing to take action to address them. In 1 Timothy 3, Paul writes regarding the qualifications of men who are called to serve the church as elders, emphasizing how important it is to evaluate if a man "manages his own household well," as an indicator of whether he can care for the church of God:

> He must be one who manages his own household well, keeping his children under control with all dignity (but if a man does not know how to manage his own household, how will he take care of the church of God?) (1 Timothy 3:4-5)

Your wisdom and instruction

A man provides guidance, support, and direction for his family and home through wisdom and instruction. It is a sobering thought for a man to consider his family will depend on him to provide wisdom and instruction, and it would be foolish to for him to think that wisdom and instruction are found within himself. All wisdom comes from God. Proverbs is a source of great wisdom, and Proverbs 2 speaks to the attainment of wisdom, explaining that wisdom is given by the Lord:

> My son, if you will receive my words and treasure my commandments within you, make your ear attentive to wisdom, incline your heart to understanding; For if you cry for discernment, lift your voice for understanding; If you seek her as silver and search for her as for hidden treasures; Then you will discern the fear of the Lord and discover the knowledge of God. For the Lord gives wisdom; From His mouth come knowledge and understanding. He stores up sound wisdom for the upright; He is a shield to those who walk in integrity, guarding the paths of justice, and He preserves the way of His godly ones. Then you will discern righteousness and justice and equity and every good course. For wisdom will enter your heart and knowledge will be pleasant to

your soul; Discretion will guard you, understanding will watch over you. (Proverbs 2:1-11)

This passage of scripture affirms that it is in walking humbly in relationship with God that you will find wisdom, knowledge, discernment, and understanding. Your disciplined practice of praying without ceasing is invaluable. James 1:5 instructs you to pray for wisdom, saying, "But if any of you lacks wisdom, let him ask of God, who gives to all generously and without reproach, and it will be given to him."

Wisdom is necessary for instructing, training, and disciplining your children. Parents are admonished to train up their children in the way they should go (Proverbs 22:6), and Deuteronomy 6 describes the persistent diligence of parents teaching and instructing their children daily, in all circumstances and by many means.

These words, which I am commanding you today, shall be on your heart. You shall teach them diligently to your sons and shall talk of them when you sit in your house and when you walk by the way and when you lie down and when you rise up. You shall bind them as a sign on your hand and they shall be as frontals on your forehead. You shall write them on the doorposts of your house and on your gates. (Deuteronomy 6:6-9)

PROTECTING YOUR FAMILY AND HOME

Physical Safety

A man protects his family and home from lack by seeking first the kingdom of God and His righteousness. In Matthew 6, Jesus states that our heavenly Father knows what we need for food, drink, and clothing, but we are to "seek first His kingdom and His righteousness, and all these things will be added to you" (Matthew 6:31-34). A man's family will not be threatened by physical hunger or thirst when seeking the kingdom of God is his first priority. Fathers are to teach their children to be discerning and wise regarding strangers and evil. A valuable benefit of strong discipline is the ability to set boundaries which your children will respect, and which will protect them from dangerous equipment, environments, and people.

Spiritual Safety

A man protects his family spiritually by praying for them and reinforcing the wisdom and instruction that he has provided to his household by setting standards for godly behavior and prohibiting ungodly behavior. Examples of what scripture says are out-of-bounds behaviors can be found in Ephesians 5, where Paul writes:

> But immorality or any impurity or greed must not even be named among you, as is proper among saints; and there must be no filthiness and silly talk, or coarse jesting, which are not fitting, but rather giving of thanks. For this you know with certainty, that no immoral or impure person or covetous man, who is an idolater, has an inheritance in the kingdom of Christ and God. (Ephesians 5:3-5)

In Psalm 141, David prayed, "Set a guard, O Lord, over my mouth; Keep watch over the door of my lips" (Psalm 141:3). The Christian man pays attention to the words which he speaks and which others in his household speak, and *how* they are spoken, understanding the power of the tongue from James 3.

> And the tongue is a fire, the very world of iniquity; the tongue is set among our members as that which defiles the entire body, and sets on fire the course of our life, and is set on fire by hell. (James 3:6)

Guarding the members of his household from the unbridled evil which is casually transmitted over the television, computers, tablets, and cell phones, must be a top priority for a father and husband. Limiting overall access to electronic devices shows compassion and protection for family members as well; overuse of these devices is detrimental for the development of social and relational skills.

Emotional safety

A man who loves and cares for his family will protect their emotional safety by guarding his mouth, and he will speak with gentleness toward his wife and children. Paul instructs the men in Philippi to "Let your gentle spirit be known to all men" (Philippians 4:5). Proverbs 16 says, "Pleasant words are a honeycomb, sweet to the soul and healing to the bones" (Proverbs 16:24).

An element of loving your wife sacrificially is setting aside your expectations of how you would expect your wife to speak and act toward you. Remember, she is not a man! You would not want her to be like, or to act like, a man; and yet, women are infinitely mysterious to men. It is unreasonable to expect her to act in a way that would always be comfortable and familiar to you, as a man. It is important to understand this, and in 1 Peter 3:7 husbands are admonished to "live with your wives in an understanding way, as with someone weaker, since she is a woman; and show her honor as a fellow heir of the grace of life, so that your prayers will not be hindered." This means not allowing frustration and impatience to determine how you speak and respond to her, but to instead be gracious and kind in your speech.

Multiple times in scripture, fathers are instructed to restrain their harsh responses, and, instead, be gentle with their children. Scripture admonishes fathers to be thoughtful and caring toward their children.

> Fathers, do not provoke your children to anger, but bring them up in
> the discipline and instruction of the Lord. (Ephesians 6:4)

> Fathers, do not exasperate your children, so that they will not lose heart.
> (Colossians 3:21)

Financial Safety

A man protects his family and home by managing the household finances with prudence and wisdom, and by being disciplined in spending. Hebrews 13:5 instructs us to "Make sure that your character is free from the love of money, being content with what you have." Spending beyond your means is guaranteed to lead to unhappiness and misery, and is known as a leading cause for breaking up families. Debt should be avoided, as it is known to be a path to slavery, as noted in Proverbs 22:7, "The rich rules over the poor, and the borrower becomes the lender's slave." This often means saying *no* to desirable and enjoyable purchases that many of your friends and coworkers consume without a second thought. Unrestrained spending in the short term often results in financial destitution over many years. Romans 13 provides wise instruction, saying, "Owe nothing to anyone except to love one another; for he who loves his neighbor has fulfilled the law" (Romans 13:8).

Work hard, spend wisely, give generously, and trust God, knowing that at all times you are in a place of entire dependence on Him!

PLANNING FOR YOUR FAMILY AND HOME

Life Planning

Household stewardship involves planning for the life of your family. This is a dynamic process which must adapt to new and unexpected circumstances, opportunities, and tragedies as time moves on. If married, these are important discussions to have with your wife, and for the two of you to spend time in prayer about together. All of your planning should be held loosely, as you cannot control or predict the future, and you must be ready to adjust your plans to correlate with new information as you live and learn through each day. The book of James warns of the pride and arrogance of making plans for the future and being confident in them:

> Come now, you who say, "Today or tomorrow we will go to such and
> such a city, and spend a year there and engage in business and make a

profit." Yet you do not know what your life will be like tomorrow. You are just a vapor that appears for a little while and then vanishes away. Instead, you ought to say, "If the Lord wills, we will live and also do this or that." But as it is, you boast in your arrogance; all such boasting is evil. (James 4:13-16)

As God's steward, He has plans and purpose for your life. It is good to ponder and to plan for what might be probable outcomes in the future, while holding those plans loosely before the Lord. Seek His will, and trust His direction. Proverbs 16:9 describes this, saying, "The mind of man plans his way, but the Lord directs his steps."

Things to consider and plan for include: is there a church nearby with which you can worship, fellowship, and grow spiritually? Are you close to family and friends with whom you want the opportunity to spend time and build relationships? What is the proximity to your work? Are there desirable schools and shopping nearby?

Home Planning

As the steward of your household, you will consider and evaluate the needs your family has in a home. As a family moves through the seasons of their life, their home needs evolve. A small apartment or 2-bedroom starter home may be the perfect fit for newlyweds, but four children later, you might feel the squeeze! Can you move to a new, larger home? That depends on how well you have planned for your changing needs! Planning consists of caring well for your current home so that it retains or grows in value, and resisting the urge to spend money and purchase items which are unnecessary. This discipline will allow you to save money toward the purchase of a larger home many years ahead. Maintaining your home means you plan for the needed repairs or replacement of major appliances and building components, like roofing, siding, and windows on the exterior of the home, and flooring, paint, appliances, and fixtures on the interior. Caring well for your home as a steward of God proves your readiness to be entrusted with more resources.

Financial Planning

Stewardship of your household includes the spectrum of short, mid, and long-term financial planning. Collaborating with your wife to establish a monthly budget to manage your income and expenses is an essential process of good stewardship. That budget is the first step of planning how your family will meet each 30-day short-term financial goal, paying all necessary expenses with sufficient income, and without borrowing. Just to be clear on this issue, using a credit card is borrowing, and carrying any balance is *very* costly because of outrageous interest rates. If you choose to use a credit card, discipline yourself to pay off the balance on each statement so you don't have to pay interest. Many people can be successful with doing this month after month. But be aware that it's a fast and slippery slope to significant debt when you begin to carry a balance on the credit card. Using a debit card connected with your bank account is often a much better option, as the debit card enables you to make digital transactions, but without borrowing someone else's money.

Building a plan for generosity into that monthly budget is an important act of obedience and submission to scriptural instruction. 1 John says that Christians should be ready to help our brothers who need any worldly goods (1 John 3:17). Generosity is a valuable characteristic for preparing us for greater stewardship; Proverbs 11 contrasts the outcome for the generous and for the stingy, saying,

> There is one who scatters, and yet increases all the more, and there is one who withholds what is justly due, and yet it results only in want. The generous man will be prosperous, and he who waters will himself be watered. (Proverbs 11:24-25)

The consistent practice of giving is the most important first step. A consistent, cheerful, weekly offering to the Lord is the foundation for exponential growth over time. What is the right amount to plan for generous giving? The correct answer to this question is not a dollar amount, but it is a *responsive awareness*. Paul, writing in 2 Corinthians, gives these instructions for how the church at Corinth was to prepare a gift for the ministry:

> Now this I say, he who sows sparingly will also reap sparingly, and he
> who sows bountifully will also reap bountifully. Each one must do just
> as he has purposed in his heart, not grudgingly or under compulsion,
> for God loves a cheerful giver. (2 Corinthians 9:6-7)

Mid-term financial goals include larger expenses which are semi-annual or annual, such as auto, home, and life insurance, property taxes, and intermittent major repair or replacement expenses.

Long-term financial goals should include future home and vehicle purchases and retirement planning. Insurance planning may avoid catastrophic financial burdens in case of health issues or the death of you or your wife. As a family moves through the stages of life and further along the path of aging, long-term estate planning is an important step in thoughtfully determining how the resources God has entrusted to you will be managed and allocated in the event of your death. Proverbs 13:22 references estate planning, saying, "A good man leaves an inheritance to his children's children."

Spiritual Planning

Spiritual planning for your family and home dovetails with protecting your family with spiritual safety. We should be thoughtful and deliberate in our personal discipline of prayer and Bible study. What time will you set aside each day for this practice (Colossians 4:2, Deuteronomy 11:18-23)? How will you implement your routine of one-on-one teaching and spiritual instruction for your children (Deuteronomy 6:6-9, Ephesians 6:4)? What does weekly, consistent engagement in congregate worship and fellowship look like for your family (Hebrews 10:23-25)?

An often overlooked element of spiritual planning and care for your family and home is simple transparency before each other daily. Parents make plenty of mistakes, and they even sin against each other and their children. A parent's honest confession of sin against their child, coupled with a sincere appeal for forgiveness, will make an indelible impression upon that child's faith journey. To have been the recipient of their father's humble modeling of contrition and repentance is a treasured lesson of the grace-filled life that is available to them through Christ. Other than Christ's sacrifice, there is no greater instructive example than this for a child to learn how to rebuild the broken relationships they are certain to experience throughout life. Parents have powerful opportunities to model, teach, and discuss with their children the truths of the transformed life under the reign of God.

A LIVING EXAMPLE

Ethan watched as Connor hit the ball off the tee, ran to first base, and then wandered twenty feet into right field to sit down and pick a bright yellow dandelion. He smiled and said, "Jonathon, half of me is feeling anxious about these disciplines of stewardship, and what seems to be an enormous stewarding responsibility. The other half of me is at peace. It's exciting to see and learn a framework for living out the gospel in my family and home, while knowing I'm probably going to fall flat on my face way too often! I am confident that as Leesh and I begin this stewardship adventure, God is delighted to see us taking action in our faith walk. I believe He smiles on us in the same way that I smile on Connor, as he clumsily does his best at tee ball these first weeks."

Jonathon laughed out loud and gave Ethan a hearty slap on the back, saying, "That is such a great parallel, Ethan! I'm sure that Connor is experiencing some moments of frustration and feeling overwhelmed as he tries to figure out how the rules work, what he should do and when he should do it. But when he looks up here and sees you smiling down at him, that helps to ease the frustration, and assures him you are pleased with him, regardless of the clumsiness. Your smile toward him now is a great way for him to see you illustrating and modeling how God will smile on him in future years, as he is struggling with these same disciplines of stewardship. Grace is catchy in that way!"

Both men laughed, and found themselves encouraged by the thought of God being delighted with them, despite their struggles and stumbles.

Discussion and Discipline

- There are many aspects to providing for your family and home. In which areas do you that see you are practicing those disciplines consistently? Do these areas of practice surprise you, or are they areas you had never thought about before? What steps can you take now to move into these stewardship disciplines?

- Many men think only of protecting their family and home regarding physical safety, protecting against bad guys, harm, injuries, etc. Is it a new thought for you to consider protection for your family and home in spiritual matters? What is one decision you can make today, and practice consistently, to increase spiritual safety for your family and home?

- Short, mid, and long-term planning for your family and home is a very broad spectrum. A man's process for stewarding in this area follows a sequence of progression in that same order: short, mid, and then long-term planning. It can take a while for the realities of mid and long-term planning to work into a man's awareness. Unfortunately, that delay sometimes leaves families unprepared for difficult and/or unexpected events. Can you choose one goal for each area of planning to address today? Can you choose one short-term goal, one mid-term goal, and one long-term goal?

- Ethan recognized the potential for himself to get caught up in performance demands, as he contemplated moving forward with developing and practicing these disciplines of stewardship; he knew that would lead to frustration and being overwhelmed. Seeing himself through the eyes of a loving heavenly Father, who found delight in his clumsy initial stewardship efforts, helped to relieve that anxiety. Do you tend to be performance-based and get stressed out with new challenges, or are you motivated, but relaxed, about getting started, allowing yourself to be imperfect and have the time to practice and improve?

Chapter Fifteen

"One Another" Stewardship

Life, Fellowship, and Worship Together

E than and Jonathon met earlier than usual for breakfast this Saturday morning. Jonathon was meeting later that morning with Anthony, who was a mutual friend of theirs. Anthony was a member of their church and took part in a men's Bible study with Ethan and Jonathon.

Earlier that week on Wednesday, at the men's Bible study, Anthony had shared with the group that he was needing their help and support. When Anthony received the good news of the gospel six years ago, he was deep in the grips of alcohol. When he placed his faith in Jesus, he wholeheartedly denied Self and took up his cross daily to follow Him. Anthony's story was a beautiful picture of redemption and a slow restoration of the relationships which had been damaged or broken by the sin of his addiction. But this week, Anthony had shared with the men in the Bible study that the prior six months had been increasingly stressful at his work, and he had allowed anxiety and awful thoughts to have free rein in his mind. This led up to the prior weekend when his wife, Kari, was visiting family out of town. After a terrible Friday at work, Anthony drove to a liquor store that was an old haunt of his. It was the next day, as he was burying the empty bottles deep in the outside trash container, before he came to himself and realized the significance of what he had done. Anthony drove to Jonathon's home to confess his sin and to ask for help. He knew what he had done would be devastating to his wife; he wasn't sure she would even be willing to continue in their marriage.

When Anthony shared this story with the men in the Bible study, he told them how Jonathon and Marie had come alongside him and Kari to love and support them through the painful times ahead. After confessing and unloading this hard story, Anthony had wept when the men, together with one movement and voice, stood up to surround him and pray for him.

After ordering breakfast, Ethan spoke to Jonathon about Anthony. "My heart was breaking on Wednesday as Anthony told us what was going on; first, for him, knowing how destructive alcoholism is, and second, for both him and for Kari, needing to work through broken trust and figure out how to feel safe going forward in their marriage."

"It is really difficult, and will continue to be difficult for a long time; it is so painful for both of them," Jonathon nodded in agreement. "In many ways, it is too heavy a burden for either of them to carry alone. We know that, being made in the image of God, healthy relationships with others are essential for us to manage and navigate the hard challenges of life. That's why we, the church, are instructed by the Bible and taught by the Holy Spirit to love and care for one another, to bear one another's burdens, and to encourage and strengthen one another. In fact, today, that's what we were going to talk about: "One Another" Stewardship. How do we steward our relationships with each other in the body of Christ? What does it look like to share life together, to fellowship together, and to worship together? Anthony's story is our story, and we all need each other as members of the body of Christ."

REMEMBER – LOVE IS FIRST

> Jesus answered, "The foremost [commandment] is, 'Hear, O Israel! The Lord our God is one Lord; and you shall love the Lord your God with all your heart, and with all your soul, and with all your mind, and with all your strength.' The second is this, 'You shall love your neighbor as yourself.' There is no other commandment greater than these." (Mark 12:29-31)

Since God created man in His image, relationships are at the center of a man's purposeful and meaningful engagement with the world around him. "One Another" stewardship is the intentional and responsible management, care, and protection of relationships with other believers, with whom one regularly worships and fellowships.

LIFE TOGETHER

Loving one another

The disciplines of "One Another" Stewardship, like all Christian disciplines, are directly bound to, and rooted in the foremost "One Another" discipline, that of loving one another. The night before His crucifixion, Jesus gave this command to His disciples:

> "A new commandment I give to you, that you love one another, even as I have loved you, that you also love one another. By this all men will know that you are My disciples, if you have love for one another." (John 13:34-35)

Jesus' command to love one another is so central to the Christian faith (the narrow way) that He said our love for one another will be the hallmark for all men to observe and know that we are Jesus' disciples. The proof of our discipleship is not the frequency of going to church, that we pray in public, the bumper stickers on our car, or the lack of curse words in our conversation. All men will know we are Jesus' disciples when they observe how we love other Christians.

What does it look like to love one another? We have to go no further than Paul's portrait of love found in 1 Corinthians 13.

> Love is patient, love is kind and is not jealous; love does not brag and is not arrogant, does not act unbecomingly; it does not seek its own, is not provoked, does not take into account a wrong suffered, does not rejoice in unrighteousness, but rejoices with the truth; bears all things, believes all things, hopes all things, endures all things. (1 Corinthians 13:4-7)

These are the characteristics demonstrated by Christians who love one another in accordance with Jesus' command. Paul's firm instruction, specifically to the men of the church in Corinth and found in 1 Corinthians 16:13-14, echoes this command, saying, "Be on the alert, stand firm in the faith, act like men, be strong. Let all that you do be done in love." Having looked carefully at this new commandment that Jesus gives us, we should also speak plainly about the real life challenges of obeying the commandment. It may seem to us that Jesus must have meant that we are to love one another in a general sense. We might wrongly think in those circumstances when another Christian is acting badly, disagreeably, or hurtfully toward us, Jesus cannot expect us to just go on loving them! That would be like saying, *love one another until you find out your Christian brother is a broken, sinful person who is a desperate recipient of Christ's redemption.* But every one of us is in that exact condition; we are broken, sinful, utterly impotent regarding righteousness, and desperate recipients of redemption in Christ through God's bountiful grace! Jesus commands us to love one another as He has loved us. It is only when we humbly recognize that Jesus loved us in our broken, sinful condition that we can walk in a manner worthy of God's calling in our relationships with one another. The apostle Paul instructed the church at Ephesus about this humility which should frame our relationships with each other:

> Therefore I, the prisoner of the Lord, implore you to walk in a manner
> worthy of the calling with which you have been called, with all humility
> and gentleness, with patience, showing tolerance for one another in
> love, being diligent to preserve the unity of the Spirit in the bond of
> peace. (Ephesians 4:1-3)

Our relationships with one another are to be characterized by humility and gentleness when we have differing viewpoints, and we should show patience toward one another when our expectations are disappointed or we somehow feel disappointed by the other. Showing tolerance for one another in love means not having to submit to your compulsions to insist on why you are right and the other person must be wrong. Relationships with these characteristics are not found in the world, and are a testimony to the transformative gospel of Jesus Christ.

Forgive one another

The last section in Ephesians, chapter four, continues to describe the real challenges of living in relationship, and to prescribe the manner in which we are to pattern our behavior toward each other. In verses 25–32 we are instructed to speak the truth to each other, be angry without sin, never give the devil an opportunity to bring destruction into our relationships, mind the words we say, never grieve the Holy Spirit, and to throw away from us all bitterness and wrath and anger and clamor and slander and malice. These are all hard disciplines to cultivate in our lives, and we will fall sadly short in our practice no matter how intensely we purpose to love as we are commanded. So Paul ends this instruction with these ultimate words: "Be kind to one another, tender-hearted, forgiving each other, just as God in Christ also has forgiven you" (Ephesians 4:32).

In Colossians, we read a similar description of how we are to relate to one another with compassion, humility, patience, and forgiveness.

> So, as those who have been chosen of God, holy and beloved, put on a heart of compassion, kindness, humility, gentleness and patience; bearing with one another, and forgiving each other, whoever has a complaint against anyone; just as the Lord forgave you, so also should you. Beyond all these things put on love, which is the perfect bond of unity. (Colossians 3:12-14)

Because we each remain so vulnerable to the brokenness of this world, and susceptible to the seductive pleasures of Self, we should live with one another in an understanding way, being kind and tender-hearted, extending to each other the same forgiveness with which we have been forgiven by God, in Christ Jesus. There will be unending opportunities and occasions for missteps, mistakes, misstatements, and even intentional hurts and disappointments between Christian brothers on this earth. Forgiveness is the essential practice of every Christian; it is not optional. Consider the Lord's Prayer, where Jesus taught His disciples to pray, "And forgive us our debts, as we also have forgiven our debtors" (Matthew 6:12).

Bearing one another's burdens

In Galatians 6, we are instructed to "bear one another's burdens." The context here follows Paul's discourse in chapter five, contrasting walking by the Spirit with carrying out the desires of the flesh, since "the flesh sets its desire against the Spirit, and the Spirit against the flesh; for these are in opposition to one another..." (Galatians 5:17). He continues then, in chapter 6, saying,

> Brethren, even if anyone is caught in any trespass, you who are spiritual, restore such a one in a spirit of gentleness; each one looking to yourself, so that you too will not be tempted. Bear one another's burdens, and thereby fulfill the law of Christ. For if anyone thinks he is something when he is nothing, he deceives himself. (Galatians 6:1-3)

To bear another's burdens here is in the context of restoring him in a spirit of gentleness after he has been "caught in any trespass." The word used in the original language is *"prolambano"*, meaning, *"to take by surprise; pass. be taken unexpectedly, be overtaken, be taken by surprise"* ((n.d.). The Online Greek Bible. Retrieved June 3, 2024, from https://www.greekbible.com/galatians/6/1). Coming alongside one who is suffering under a great load of guilt and sorrow after being overtaken by sin and lifting a portion of that weight from his shoulders in gentle restoration, is an act of love. While it's not possible to eliminate the real consequences of sin, even after repentance, to have a brother walk alongside you through the painful days in the future, strengthens the inner man and fortifies the commitment to righteous living. Along with encouragement and counsel, a godly friend gives reminders of the truth found in scripture, against which one can measure the deceptive thoughts and lofty speculations raised up against the knowledge of God.

Romans 15 also couples the act of bearing the weaknesses of others with denying self, saying, "Now we who are strong ought to bear the weaknesses of those without strength and not just please our [Selves]. Each of us is to please his neighbor for his good, to his edification" (Romans 15:1-2). In the previous chapter (Romans 14), attention is brought to what some call *principles of conscience*, those things which are not necessarily right or wrong, but each one needs to consider and determine one's own conviction regarding eating certain foods or drink, or observing certain days. Romans 14:1 begins the topic with the admonition to "accept the one who is weak in faith, but not for the purpose of passing judgment on his opinions." Bearing your brother's weaknesses means not needing to win the argument over differing views on these principles of conscience, being careful not to put a stumbling block in his way, and pursuing "the things which make for peace and the building up of one another" (Romans 14:19).

Connected With One Another

Christians are to steward their relationships with one another with an understanding of God's design of our interdependence upon each other. The Bible refers to believers as being one body in Christ. This shows the importance of relationship for man's well-being, and especially for those who are restored to right relationship with God. Paul writes to the church at Corinth, comparing the church with the physical human body:

> For even as the body is one and yet has many members, and all the members of the body, though they are many, are one body, so also is Christ. For by one Spirit we were all baptized into one body, whether Jews or Greeks, whether slaves or free, and we were all made to drink of one Spirit. For the body is not one member, but many. If the foot says, "Because I am not a hand, I am not a part of the body," it is not for this reason any the less a part of the body. And if the ear says, "Because I am not an eye, I am not a part of the body," it is not for this reason any the less a part of the body. If the whole body were an eye, where would the hearing be? If the whole were hearing, where would the sense of smell be? But now God has placed the members, each one of them, in the body, just as He desired. If they were all one member, where would the body be? But now there are many members, but one body. And the eye cannot say to the hand, "I have no need of you"; or again the head to the feet, "I have no need of you." On the contrary, it is much truer that the members of the body which seem to be weaker are necessary; and those members of the body which we deem less honorable, on these we bestow more abundant honor,

and our less presentable members become much more presentable, whereas our more presentable members have no need of it. But God has so composed the body, giving more abundant honor to that member which lacked, so that there may be no division in the body, but that the members may have the same care for one another. And if one member suffers, all the members suffer with it; if one member is honored, all the members rejoice with it. Now you are Christ's body, and individually members of it. (1 Corinthians 12:12-27)

As we are one body, Jesus is the head, as described in Colossians 1:17-18, which says, "He [Jesus] is before all things, and in Him all things hold together. He is also head of the body, the church; and He is the beginning, the firstborn from the dead, so that He Himself will come to have first place in everything."

This illustration of the body of Christ shows how essential and valuable our differences are. Each member serves the interests of the body with their particular talents, while celebrating and appreciating the unique talents of other members of the body. It is in this way that the church, the body of Christ, is wonderfully designed differently than any other type of organization. What every Christian has in common is the headship, or lordship, of Christ. The headship of Christ is the single factor that enables the potential for the church to be "perfected in unity," as Jesus prayed in John 17:20-23. Their differences actually bind them together uniquely, and each one supports and strengthens the other members of the same body. The church is an intentionally designed single entity (the body) that is composed of many different parts (unique people).

FELLOWSHIP TOGETHER

Serve One Another

Paul writes to the Galatian church, saying:

For you were called to freedom, brethren; only do not turn your freedom into an opportunity for the flesh, but through love serve one another. For the whole Law is fulfilled in one word, in the statement, "You shall love your neighbor as yourself." (Galatians 5:13-14)

Spurred on by our love for one another, we are called to serve one another as well. That can certainly be gifts of service to help individual members in the church who are in need (home repairs, help with projects, caring for children), but it also means to serve one another in the context of worship, fellowship, and ministry settings. The church gathers together for worship, prayer, and Biblical instruction regularly; and it is dependent primarily upon members of the body of Christ to serve one another for different aspects of those structured gatherings.

These places of service to one another include hospitality work: greeting and welcoming, ushering, and preparing and serving food. Many serve in roles of teaching and preaching, use of technology, and administration of projects. Worship services benefit from those who share their talents of playing musical instruments or singing and everyone can appreciate the dependability of those who clean and organize, and who plan for various activities through the seasons of the year.

Sometimes Christians won't offer to serve because they are not confident in their ability to do the task. Because of fear or pride, they are not willing to take the risk of serving. For most people, a simple willingness to serve is the greatest factor for success, and many discover their gifts in the process of serving consistently.

As a final note on serving one another, look at the words written in 1 Peter 4:7-11. Verse 10 reads, "As each one has received a special gift, employ it in serving one another as good stewards of the manifold grace of God." You may not know what your special gift is that you should employ in serving others as a good steward, but the first test of your faith is your *willingness* to serve others, so serve *somewhere*!

Encourage One Another

Every man needs encouragement from other godly men. That daily encouragement in truth shields us from sin. Hebrews instructs us in the critical role that relational accountability plays in protecting us from the deceit of sin, and the importance of continuing to assemble together in fellowship:

Let us hold fast the confession of our hope without wavering, for He who promised is faithful; and let us consider how to stimulate one another to love and good deeds, not forsaking our own assembling together, as is the habit of some, but encouraging one another; and all the more as you see the day drawing near. (Hebrews 10:23-25)

Take care, brethren, that there not be in any one of you an evil, unbelieving heart that falls away from the living God. But encourage one another day after day, as long as it is still called "Today," so that none of you will be hardened by the deceitfulness of sin. (Hebrews 3:12-13)

When isolated and left alone with our own thoughts, the devil is relentless in his deceptive schemes, twisting truth into deception and infecting our thoughts with the wickedness of pride. Without other honest and loving Christians encouraging us in our faith consistently, we are in danger of becoming hardened by the deceitfulness of sin. We are instructed to "encourage one another day after day." One may hear the deceptive thought rolling around in your mind, questioning, *do I really need relationship with anyone?* It is time to destroy a stronghold! That thought needs to be taken captive to the obedience of Jesus Christ. Stay connected in relationship, and encourage one another day after day, as long as it is still called "*Today!*"

Sharpen One Another

To sharpen one another refers to a particular vein of encouragement for one another, that of challenging and stimulating one another to do more, go further, and stretch higher in our faith, our love, our care, and our spiritual growth. This familiar proverb compares the sharpening of iron with the sharpening of men: "Iron sharpens iron, so one man sharpens another" (Proverbs 27:17).

Mind you, when iron is sharpened, it requires great friction, and heat is always involved. Both friction and heat are factors, whether the imagery here is of two blades running their sharp edges against each other, or of one blade being heated in the furnace and then, when softened, struck with the iron hammer to shape and sharpen its edge. Christian men need to develop their capacity to receive constructive criticism without becoming defensive. This is called being resilient. Resilience is an important characteristic of maturity.

Becoming skilled in the practice of thinking critically and having rational conversation are important aspects of growing up and maturing in Christ. In Paul's letter to the Ephesian church, in chapter 4, he describes this process of maturing in faith through relationships with other Christians, being equipped for the work of service, attaining to the unity of the faith and of the knowledge of Christ to a mature man. God intends for this maturing and sharpening to happen through relationships with other men, as Paul continues to outline the process, elements, and outcomes of this maturing.

> As a result, we are no longer to be children, tossed here and there by waves and carried about by every wind of doctrine, by the trickery of men, by craftiness in deceitful scheming; but speaking the truth in love, we are to grow up in all aspects into Him who is the head, even Christ, from whom the whole body, being fitted and held together by what every joint supplies, according to the proper working of each individual part, causes the growth of the body for the building up of itself in love. (Ephesians 4:14-16)

Romans 15:14 is straightforward in saying that we are to be "filled with all knowledge and able also to admonish one another" and a more direct admonition is given in Hebrews 10, saying,

> Let us hold fast the confession of our hope without wavering, for He who promised is faithful; and let us consider how to stimulate one another to love and good deeds... (Hebrews 10:23-24)

This is the challenge for each man – *how might we consider stimulating our brother to love and good deeds?* Remember, every discipline of stewardship grows and develops from, and is motivated by, love for God and love for others. Let that be our guardrail for the actions we might consider, to provide that stimulation for one another.

WORSHIP TOGETHER

The Christian church has traditionally gathered weekly, typically on Sundays, for an organized time of corporate worship. The day of the week, or specific time of that day, are not important; scripture prescribes neither a specific day or time for corporate worship. What is important to understand is that scripture *does* prescribe that believers organize and assemble for corporate worship under the watchful care and oversight of qualified elders as shepherds. In the book of Hebrews, the writer encourages each person's regular engagement with corporate assembly, while noting those who are disobedient, saying:

> Let us hold fast the confession of our hope without wavering, for He who promised is faithful; and let us consider how to stimulate one another to love and good deeds, not forsaking our own assembling together, as is the habit of some, but encouraging one another; and all the more as you see the day drawing near. (Hebrews 10:23-25)

It is in the context of corporate assembly and worship that qualified elders administer the sacraments, preach the Word, and provide instruction and discipline. Corporate and public song, praise, prayer, and gifts of offering forge a multitude of individuals into the singular functioning body of Christ, being "fitted and held together by what every joint supplies, according to the proper working of each individual part, causes the growth of the body for the building up of itself in love" (Ephesians 4:16). Jesus petitions the Father for the church, praying:

> I do not ask on behalf of these alone, but for those also who believe in Me through their word; that they may all be one; even as You, Father, are in Me and I in You, that they also may be in Us, so that the world may believe that You sent Me. (John 17:20-21)

This unity, or oneness of the church, is forged, strengthened and shown to the world through regular corporate assembly. Jesus said, "By this all men will know that you are

My disciples, if you have love for one another." It is in the practice of regular corporate assembly that the world can observe Christians in this level of relationship and loving one another.

Receiving Teaching with One Another

As the church gathers in corporate assembly, qualified elders preach and teach the Word, bringing instruction, encouragement, and understanding from scripture to the church, and administer the sacraments (1 Timothy 3:1-7, Titus 1:6-9, Acts 2:41-42, Acts 14:27, Acts 20:7, Hebrews 13:17, 1 Corinthians 11:23-34).

Singing and Praising God with One Another

Through songs and singing, we are taught truth, and express thankfulness to God, as stated in Colossians 3.

> Let the word of Christ richly dwell within you, with all wisdom teaching and admonishing one another with psalms and hymns and spiritual songs, singing with thankfulness in your hearts to God. (Colossians 3:16)

In Acts 16:25, Paul and Silas were holding the first worship service in a jail (they had been arrested for preaching Christ), and at midnight they were "praying and singing hymns of praise to God." Let us be very clear about something, singing is neither a masculine nor a feminine activity. It is an expression of worship, passion, and teaching that God designed for mankind when He created man in His image. Many men have been deceived and believed the lie, that "real men" don't sing. This is a speculation that is raised up against the knowledge of God and it stands as an unholy fortress of Self-protection within the minds of men. Men need to destroy these fortresses and take captive every thought to the obedience of Jesus Christ. Men are called to sing and to worship, as described in Ephesians 5:19, James 5:13, Matthew 26:30, Hebrews 2:12, and endless Old Testament references!

Prayer With One Another

Christians gathering together in corporate prayer is a hallmark of the church in all circumstances, in times of persecution and tribulation, and in times of great need or rejoicing. From the very beginning of the church, following Christ's ascension, the church has fastidiously gathered to pray, as recorded in Acts 2:

> So then, those who had received his word were baptized; and that day there were added about three thousand souls. They were continually devoting themselves to the apostles' teaching and to fellowship, to the breaking of bread and to prayer. (Acts 2:41-42)

Men are specifically instructed to pray together in corporate gatherings, as 1 Timothy 2:8 says, "Therefore I want the men in every place to pray, lifting up holy hands, without wrath and dissension." And James 5 calls for corporate prayer, specifically by the elders of the church, in response to a request made by a church member who is sick:

> Is anyone among you sick? Then he must call for the elders of the church and they are to pray over him, anointing him with oil in the name of the Lord; and the prayer offered in faith will restore the one who is sick, and the Lord will raise him up, and if he has committed sins, they will be forgiven him. (James 5:14–15)

It is helpful to contrast what Paul instructs in 1 Thessalonians 5:17 when he writes, "pray without ceasing" with the multitude of other references elsewhere for groups, gatherings, and assemblies of Christians to pray together. Remember that 1 Thessalonians was written to the church at Thessalonica, not to an individual. So, it stands to reason that the instruction to pray without ceasing was instruction for all members of the church, as individuals. On the other hand, it is not possible to continue to "corporately" pray without ceasing. Once you separate and go your individual ways, you can no longer corporately pray. That is why it is reasonable to consider 1 Thessalonians 5:17 to be instructive primarily to each individual man. In contrast, corporate prayer is unique from personal prayer in that it reflects a mutual joining together as one voice in prayer, whether there are two or three, or a multitude of Christians praying together (Matthew 18:19-20, Acts 1:13-14, Acts 4:24, Acts 4:31, Acts 12:5, Acts 12:12).

Giving Offerings *with* One Another

Generosity, or the sharing of one's wealth with others, is an innate characteristic within man who is created in God's image. However, with the rise of Self, through pride, and the consequent separation from God, fallen man has largely lost sight of this element which is hardwired into his being. As opposed to sharing what one has with others, Self instead trains man to be greedy and endlessly accumulate resources for himself, and even to covet what others have obtained.

Once Self is denied, and the truth of scripture begins the process of transforming the man through the renewing of his mind, the man has opportunity to discover the amazing nature of God's economy. In Acts 20:35, Paul reminds the church of the words of Jesus, who said, "It is more blessed to give than to receive." Here, the word *blessed* is the Greek word *"makarios"*, which means, *"fortunate, good (in a position of favor), happy (feelings associated with receiving God's favor)" (NIV Exhaustive Concordance Dictionary. Copyright © 2015 by Zondervan).* Giving actually generates happy feelings, because we know we receive God's favor when we give. This illustrates the nature of generosity being hardwired into our being through creation.

In both the Old Testament and the New Testament, scripture instructs willing generosity and describes God's favor upon those who are generous:

> Honor the Lord from your wealth and from the first of all your produce. (Proverbs 3:9)

> Since we have gifts that differ according to the grace given to us, each of us is to exercise them accordingly: ...he who gives, with liberality; he who leads, with diligence; he who shows mercy, with cheerfulness. ...Be devoted to one another in brotherly love; give preference to one another in honor; ...contributing to the needs of the saints... (Romans 12:6–13)

In the Old Testament, laws were given to instruct the Israelites in the required practice of tithing. The word tithe means "a tenth". The people of God were to give a tenth
of their crops and livestock (cows, goats, lambs) for the service of the tabernacle (the
building structure where God dwelled) and the support of the Levites (the tribe which
was responsible for the tabernacle) and the priests. There were also additional required
tithes for other purposes. The death of Jesus on the cross fulfilled the requirements of
the Law, and there are no similar commands for the specific practice of tithing to be
found in the New Testament of the Bible. However, the New Testament clearly models
the sharing of gifts in and through the corporate assembly of the organized church
for the financial support of those called to vocational ministry to the church, and for
the sharing of resources among those in the church who are in need (Hebrews 13:16,
Romans 12:13, 1 Corinthians 9:7, 2 Corinthians 8:1–9:15). Galatians 6:6 provides
specific instruction to give corporately for the support of pastors or elders, saying, "The
one who is taught the word is to share all good things with the one who teaches him."

A man's disposition, as he gives, is a concern for God; we read in 2 Corinthians 9:

> Now this I say, he who sows sparingly will also reap sparingly, and he
> who sows bountifully will also reap bountifully. Each one must do just
> as he has purposed in his heart, not grudgingly or under compulsion,
> for God loves a cheerful giver. (2 Corinthians 9:6-7)

We see here that two questions are answered concerning a man's decision to be
generous. How much should a man give? *You must do (give) just as you have purposed
in your heart!* How should I feel about giving? *Cheerful!*

Paul describes a practice for corporate giving at the church in Corinth, which may
sound familiar to many modern churches. He writes in 1 Corinthians 16:1-2, "Now
concerning the collection for the saints, as I directed the churches of Galatia, so do
you also. On the first day of every week each one of you is to put aside and save, as
he may prosper, so that no collections be made when I come." Of course, this again is
not prescriptive, but it shows a model of routine, consistent, and cheerful giving in the
congregate setting.

SPIRITUAL SAFETY, SUPPORT, AND PROTECTION

After studying the "One Another" stewardship of scripture, Ethan found that he had grown in appreciation for the church. He could only imagine how difficult and painful the circumstances were for Anthony and his wife right now, but it would be unthinkable and feel impossible to face such devastation without the love and support of the body of Christ. It would be terrifying to be so alone.

Ethan and Jonathon spent the rest of their time that morning in the restaurant booth, praying together for Anthony and Kari, for each other and their families, and for the men of their church. They prayed God would continue to forge strong, encouraging relationships within and between the men of the body of Christ, and that they would lead their families each day on the narrow way with courage, love, and humility.

Discussion and Discipline

- Consider what scripture teaches us about our Life Together, and how Jesus said that all men will know we are His disciples if we have love for one another. Are you "all in" as you worship and fellowship with other men of the church? Or do you hold back and protect your vulnerabilities from being exposed in close relationships? How can you practice the relationships scripture describes for the men of the church?

- As we Fellowship Together, it seems critical to first practice denying Self and embrace the call to serve one another. This posture of humility in our relationships with others is a beautiful reflection of our place of entire dependence on God. If instead we protect Self and seek our own benefit, we will never kneel to wash the feet of others. Are there ways you can begin to practice the serving of others?

- Men often overlook opportunities to encourage other men. Self works overtime to keep men isolated from each other. Encouraging relationships are critical in God's design for your life. The best way to release the grip of Self that keeps you in isolation is to step forward and be the encourager of other men. How would a practice of encouraging other men change your view of the body of Christ? Can you think of several men right now to whom you might give encouragement in the next few days?

- Some men view corporate worship with the church like any other public event, such as a concert or a sporting event. But scripture is clear that when Christians gather: 1) Jesus is there with them, and 2) They are each unique members of one body of Christ. Do you see yourself as a member of the body of Christ? How about those who sit near you at worship? Do you see them as members of the same body of Christ? How is that different from gathering at a public event, like a concert?

- Singing is usually a significant part of worship. Do you allow yourself to worship God through song and praise? Do you feel too Self-conscious to sing out loud? If so, consider discussing this with a trusted brother in Christ; ask if he may have insight on steps you can take to be less Self-focused and more Christ-focused in worship. Follow-up with him to report on your progress.

- From Genesis to Revelation, giving is an integral part of worship, and selfless generosity is both evidence of a humble steward's sowing of seed in worship of God, and a means through which God blesses that planted seed to produce a bountiful harvest for His steward. Have you experienced that cycle of sowing and harvesting through generous giving? If not, what is getting in the way of trusting God for the outcome He has designed for your life?

  A simple start to building trust in God for the finances he has entrusted to you is to take a small step. Purpose in your heart to give a small amount cheerfully, every worship service. Be consistent for three months. Pray that God will increase your capacity to trust Him with His own resources (remember, you're just a steward). After three more months, purpose in your heart to increase the small amount by another small amount. Repeat this cycle again and again. This will give you the opportunity to discover the joy of harvest, and though it will be proportionate to the seed you planted, it will still be a harvest! Over time, you will be amazed by your own joy in generosity, and by how God seems to multiply the resources He entrusts to your care. Will you commit to trusting God, and moving forward with steps to building a life of generosity?

Chapter Sixteen

Vocational Stewardship

Men are Designed to Work and Serve

E than was pounding back the pancakes he had ordered for his breakfast; he felt like he was starving today! He had completed a four-mile run that morning before he met Jonathon at the restaurant. It felt good to be getting back into shape, disciplining his body at the same time as he was learning to practice the disciplines of faith. Jonathon paused his enjoyment of what he had ordered off the Senior Lite menu and grinned at Ethan's ability to make those pancakes disappear. "Are you afraid some of them will get away from you?" he asked, as he laughed out loud.

Ethan looked up and paused mid-mouthful, then smiled, and held back a laugh while he finished chewing, and swallowed. "Sorry," he chuckled, "I suppose I am a little too focused on the appetite of my flesh this morning! I haven't had a run like that in years; it felt good to push my body harder again. But I sure got hungry!"

"There is nothing wrong with being hungry!" Jonathon smiled. "At the most basic level, hunger is a great motivator for us to get to work and do our share each day, even if it is just so that we can get food to eat. On the other hand, God calls for us, as Christians, to do our work for a higher purpose, to bring honor and glory to God. The next study area for spiritual discipline we will look at is vocational stewardship. We want to know God's heart. How does He want us to view and approach our employment and business relationships?"

ABOVE ALL ELSE, LOVE IS FIRST

> Jesus answered, "The foremost [commandment] is, 'Hear, O Israel! The Lord our God is one Lord; and you shall love the Lord your God with all your heart, and with all your soul, and with all your mind, and with all your strength.' The second is this, 'You shall love your neighbor as yourself.' There is no other commandment greater than these." (Mark 12:29-31)

Being created in the image of God, relationships are at the center of a man's purposeful and meaningful engagement with the world around him. Vocational stewardship is the intentional and responsible management, care, and protection of the relationships which revolve around our work: an employer, coworkers, customers, and vendors.

DESIGNED FOR WORK AND PRODUCTIVITY

Vocation is the word chosen for the work and productivity which a man performs. Defining the word vocation would include a purposeful focus, or particular function or station in life, and an intentional calling by God to that activity or work. Because God has designed man to be productive, no work should be seen as aimless or mindless busyness, void of meaning or value. The Christian man understands God designed him to work and be productive as a steward of the life and energy given him by God for that day, and he inclines and applies himself to the work and productivity which God places before him. He assumes responsibility for his behavior, mindful that it reflects the image of God in the relationships which are associated with his vocation.

Foremost, we are wise to understand God's design of man. In the beginning, God created mankind in His own image, and the first six days of creation are the demonstration of God's own work and productivity. After six days of working, God rested on the seventh day. Man, being made in God's image, is also designed and hard-wired for work and productivity. The first work, or vocation, given to man by God, was to fill the earth and "subdue" it; and have dominion over all living creatures upon the earth. Specifically addressed in Genesis 2, the first work of man was agricultural in focus, cultivating and managing the garden which God had planted in Eden.

> Then the Lord God formed man of dust from the ground, and breathed into his nostrils the breath of life; and man became a living being. The Lord God planted a garden toward the east, in Eden; and there He placed the man whom He had formed... Then the Lord God took the man and put him into the garden of Eden to cultivate it and keep it. (Genesis 2:7-8, 15)

In Exodus 20:9-10, God spoke specifically to the natural weekly cycle of man's working and being productive as a reflection of God's own week of work during creation, saying, "Six days you shall labor and do all your work, but the seventh day is a sabbath of the Lord your God..."

Scripture also admonishes those who are stubborn, and rebel against God's design for man's work and productivity, saying in 2 Thessalonians 3:10, "if anyone is not willing to work, then he is not to eat, either." Just as fundamental as eating is to man's daily existence, so is work and productivity important and central to man's design. Besides the actual performance of the work, the manner in which a man performs his work is of particular importance. It matters how the man serves his employer, encourages and supports his employees, and collaborates with his coworkers. The man who respects and serves the needs of his customers, and works to promote an environment of cooperation and mutual support, is a testimony to the transformative work of God in his life. We will discuss the fundamental nature of all work relationships and look at what scripture says about the manner in which we relate to others while we do our work.

SERVING THE NEEDS OF OTHERS

Vocational, or work relationships, are primarily of an economic nature, and all economic relationships involve a product or service provided to someone, by someone else. An employee serves an employer by providing time and productivity in exchange for wages. The employer serves the employee by providing them with wages for time and productivity. If either thinks that they are receiving a value that is less than what they are providing to the other, they can end the relationship or attempt to negotiate better terms.

In the same manner, a business serves customers by providing a service, or product, in exchange for a price. A customer serves the business by providing a price in exchange for a service or a product. If a customer thinks they are not receiving a quality of product or service equal to the price they are paying to the business, they can end the relationship, or offer a lower price. On the other hand, if a business thinks the product or service they are providing to customers has a higher value than the price customers are paying, they can raise the price of the product or service.

The heartbeat of economic relationships is the give and take, push and pull of the value of services, time, and products, with compensating wages and prices. With all relationships, there is a constant ebb and flow of tension and relief, risk and reward, concern and response. This process of serving one another through voluntary exchange builds strong and mutually dependent communities of people. The needs and interests of each person are met through the work and service of his neighbors.

Because serving the needs of others is the fundamental principle of this economic exchange, a man will often find that Self is prone to rear its head and demand control. Self wants to be the one served and elevated to an important position. It wants others to focus on him. When Self resists and rebels against serving others, work relationships become a real struggle. We will look to scripture to understand how one should view and approach his work, so we are prepared to recognize the enticing and deceptive voices of Self, and the devil, when they resist serving others. Then we will be equipped to destroy the strongholds of speculation that may linger in our minds, and we will take every thought captive to the obedience of Christ.

WE ARE FIRST GOD'S STEWARD

Whether in our work, or any other environment, it is always wise and obedient to the Lord to be conscientious that we have been "chosen of God," and be mindful that our behavior reflects that truth, as written to us in Colossians 3.

> So, as those who have been chosen of God, holy and beloved, put
> on a heart of compassion, kindness, humility, gentleness and patience;
> bearing with one another, and forgiving each other, whoever has a

complaint against anyone; just as the Lord forgave you, so also should you. (Colossians 3:12-13)

We are to always tend to the personal stewardship of our character and the practice of denying Self, as we follow Jesus through the activities of our workday. This prepares our heart to willingly serve others and to place their needs above our own.

One of the most direct admonitions given in the New Testament regarding work relationships is found later in the same chapter of Colossians.

Slaves, in all things obey those who are your masters on earth, not with external service, as those who merely please men, but with sincerity of heart, fearing the Lord. Whatever you do, do your work heartily, as for the Lord rather than for men, knowing that from the Lord you will receive the reward of the inheritance. It is the Lord Christ whom you serve. For he who does wrong will receive the consequences of the wrong which he has done, and that without partiality. Masters, grant to your slaves justice and fairness, knowing that you too have a Master in heaven. (Colossians 3:22 to 4:1)

This writing will not provide an exhaustive study and explanation of the economic and social structures of the Middle East cultures through the Classical era of history. But in applying the understanding of this passage to our current time, one could exchange the word *slave* for *worker* or *employee*, and exchange the word *master* for *employer* or *supervisor*. Workers are to respect and obey the direction and instruction of their employer, not just with external behavior, but with a respectful and sincere heart, since we respect and honor our Lord. We are told to work "heartily," or with high energy, as if we were directly doing this work for God. It is the Lord Christ whom we serve!

If we short-change, or take advantage of our employer, there will be consequences for our wrong behavior, whether our employer is aware of what we have done or not. Equally important, employers are to provide righteous or just treatment, and what is fair and equal in value to the services of productivity given, with the understanding that our Master (God) is always aware of how we serve and treat others.

In our work, we also serve and collaborate with coworkers, those who are neither a supervisor to us nor subordinate to us. Our relationship with them is just as important, and perhaps even more influential. To share encouragement, understanding, and support while one labors alongside another is a meaningful act of service, and can be a powerful testimony of the gospel. Because of the sheer number of hours coworkers share in common throughout each week, our coworkers have a unique view of the people we really are. We are broken men, who, because of God's great love for us, are redeemed by the blood of Jesus, who now reigns in our lives and walks with us daily.

Whether we serve in our work as an employer, as a supervisor, or as an employee, we know first and above all, we are servants and stewards of God. With our motivation and intention to first please God as we serve in our vocational stewardship, we are to daily put on a heart of compassion, kindness, humility, gentleness, and patience; bearing with one another, and forgiving each other (Colossians 3:12-13) as we serve and are productive in the work which God has placed before us.

It is sobering, and it is also an encouragement to know that God, as our Master in heaven, is always aware of how we serve Him in our service to others, and that He rewards those who are faithful in their stewardship. In Matthew 25:14-30, Jesus compares the kingdom of heaven to a master who left on a journey after entrusting his workers with an extraordinary amount of money. He gave five talents (a talent was about equal to about fifteen years of wages for a worker) to one, two to another, and one talent to the third. The one who was given five talents and the one who was given two talents went out and did business, trading with the talents they had received, earning five more talents and two more talents, respectively. But the one who had received the one talent dug a hole in the ground and hid the money.

When the master came to settle accounts with the three workers, he was pleased with the two who reported they had worked to multiply what he had given them, saying to each of them,

> "Well done, good and faithful slave. You were faithful with a few things,
> I will put you in charge of many things; enter into the joy of your
> master." (Matthew 25:21, 23)

The master was displeased, however, with the one who had hidden the money in the ground. He asked why it wasn't at least deposited in the bank so it could earn interest!

He ordered the talent to be taken away from that worker and given to the worker who now had ten talents. The next thing said by Jesus should really get our attention.

"For to everyone who has, more shall be given, and he will have an abundance; but from the one who does not have, even what he does have shall be taken away" (Matthew 25:29).

Proverbs 16:11 tells us, "A just balance and scales belong to the Lord; all the weights of the bag are His concern." The responsibility to steward the resources (time, energy, strength, objects) which He has given to us is on one side of the scales. On the other side, balancing against that stewardship is the actual productivity and work accomplished through our stewardship.

God has entrusted work to each of us, placing opportunities before us. Those who squander the opportunities and resources He entrusted to them, or who are unwilling to productively cause an increase from those resources, will have even what they do possess taken away from them. God rewards His faithful stewards and entrusts more to them for which to manage and care.

THANKFUL AND GROWING

Ethan was full of appreciation, as he reminded Jonathon that his work was the issue which had motivated him to connect with Jonathon so many months ago. "I was really clueless about the stewardship I had over my employment as a Christian man!" he exclaimed. "As I look back on that time, I can't believe how patient you were with me as I whined about not feeling any pleasure in my work. It's hard to believe that, since then, my boss has awarded me two bonuses over the last eight months, as he noticed how my productivity has picked up. I can honestly say that I've grown to appreciate the work I've been given to do. It's even more amazing that three of my coworkers have joined me on Wednesday mornings before work for a short devotional and time of prayer."

"That is outstanding, Ethan!" Jonathon said, and didn't hold back his ear-to-ear grin. "The transformation in you has been really evident, and it is so fun that I can be a part of what God is doing in your life. I hope you know that I've seen God's transforming work in my life continuing as we've been walking this narrow way together. It's a real blessing to partner with you in faith!"

"That reminds me of something, Jonathon." Ethan leaned in, as he asked, "Would you pray with me for Roger? Roger is one of the three who meets with me on Wednesday mornings for devotions and prayer. He's been a Christian most of his life, a lot like me. But he has shared with me a little about the struggles he's been having. I'm thinking I might ask him if he would like to meet outside of work once a week for a closer relationship with in-depth study and time in prayer, like you and I do each week. Do you think that would be okay to do? I sure don't feel like I'm an expert at any of this, but I know I'm excited about what God is doing in my life and I think Roger would love it!"

"I think that's a fantastic idea!" Jonathon reached over and put his hand on Ethan's shoulder, "Our goal isn't to be an expert at anything, it is simply to live and walk a transparent and humble life with God and each other. A significant part of our walk along the narrow way is to invite and welcome others to join us. Remember that Jesus gave us that very commission before He ascended to heaven, saying,

> "Go therefore and make disciples of all the nations, baptizing them in the name of the Father and the Son and the Holy Spirit, teaching them to observe all that I commanded you; and lo, I am with you always, even to the end of the age." (Matthew 28:19-20)

"Let's pray for Roger right now," continued Jonathon.

The two men turned toward their heavenly Father, as they expressed their care for Roger, and their desire for God to open Roger's eyes to see truth more clearly, and to know the joy of walking humbly with God and others each day.

Discussion and Discipline

- If man, being made in the image of God, is designed for work and productivity, why do so many men express dissatisfaction with their work, and some even refuse to work? How does scripture support your understanding of this? What is needed to change their thoughts and behavior about the stewardship of work?

- Have you been faithful with the work God has entrusted to you? Have you seen God entrust more to you after you have diligently worked to serve faithfully, and with energy?

- What thoughts or things get in the way of "living out" your faith at your place of work? What causes you to hesitate speaking frankly about God's redemption plan through Jesus' life and death on our behalf? Think of one or two small steps of courage you can take to acknowledge to your coworkers the most important element of your life, and take those steps this week!

- Talk out loud about the work and productivity which God has entrusted to you. Describe what you do and why it is important to you and/or to others. How does your work serve others, or help them with their concerns or needs?

- A great deception of the devil is to convince a man that he is a powerless victim in economic relationships, and that others are taking advantage of him, or that others are always at fault in difficult relationships. Why do you think this is an easy trap to fall into? What would be the path to seeing truth and correcting the deception?

- How does being God's steward first, before all other things, change your view on the work you do, or your relationship with your employer, employees, or customers?

Chapter Seventeen

Community Stewardship

Make Disciples of All Nations

E than wiped the sweat from his brow as he straightened up from stooping over the row of cucumber seeds he had planted, a slight groan escaping his lips, as his back resisted the change in position. This was the last row for him to finish planting in the community garden. The harvest in a few months would provide lower income neighbors with fresh produce for their table. He and Jonathon had agreed to help with the tilling and planting at the beginning of the season, and others would cultivate, weed, and water through the growing months.

Jonathon walked over from the small shed where he had just finished putting the garden tools away. "How's the old back doing?" he asked Ethan with a wry smile.

"Oh man," Ethan replied, "I'm sure glad I've been working out consistently for the last few months. But I think I found some muscles this morning that I might have missed until now! I'm gonna feel it tomorrow. But it's great to do this kind of work, especially knowing that it's going to be good for so many people."

"I feel the same way," Jonathon nodded, "and I'm ready for an early lunch! I think we're ready to go. The lunch buffet will start right about the time we get to the restaurant!"

As they each settled into the booth with their first helpings of food, they both felt an appreciation for the positive impact the community garden would have on their neighbors. Healthy vegetables and fruits are easy for many to take for granted, but when the budget stretches too thin, that's often one of the first places families cut back on expenses. Ethan and Jonathon had talked a few weeks earlier about how they could reach out to build relationships in the community, demonstrating care and the love of the Father. Helping with the community garden seemed like the perfect opportunity to live out their own testimony of God's love for all men.

"Today's work is perfect timing for our look at the next area of stewardship that God has given to us," said Jonathon, as he pulled his Bible over alongside his plate. "I think many Christian men have it in their heads that we've been given the great commission by Jesus to go into the world and make disciples, but I don't think many have a real, down-to-earth plan for obeying that command in a practical way through their daily lives. It's also really easy to get caught up in hotly contested political conflicts and social issues, forgetting that the Christian man's first allegiance is to Christ, and to steward life in a way that honors and brings glory to Him. Besides all that, in many ways, the Christian just doesn't fit into the world's mold, and that makes us stand out. Let's look at what the Bible says about stewarding our community relationships."

NEVER FORGET, LOVE IS FIRST

> Jesus answered, "The foremost [commandment] is, 'Hear, O Israel! The Lord our God is one Lord; and you shall love the Lord your God with all your heart, and with all your soul, and with all your mind, and with all your strength.' The second is this, 'You shall love your neighbor as yourself.' There is no other commandment greater than these." (Mark 12:29-31)

Being created in the image of God, relationships are at the center of a man's purposeful and meaningful engagement with the world around him. Community stewardship is the intentional and responsible management, care, and protection of relationships with neighbors in our community. Our neighbors include those we know, as well as those we have never met. As Jesus taught in the parable of the Good Samaritan (Luke 10:25-37), we choose to be a "neighbor" to all we encounter along the daily path of our lives, offering kindness and help as we choose to care for their needs above our own. This means coming alongside, to help those who are struggling with physical or mental limitations. It also includes not allowing our dog to do its business in someone else's yard, or inviting the elderly shopper behind us in the grocery store line to go ahead of us.

CIVIL RELATIONSHIPS

Perhaps the broadest scope of how the Christian man is to steward his relationships in the community is regarding civic life. This is because civil authorities institute and enforce laws that address how all men are to interact with each other through most areas of daily living. The purpose of law includes protecting the fundamental rights of citizens, regulating contracts and agreements, establishing standards for behavior and maintaining order, and resolving disputes.

As Christians, our primary citizenship is not in this world, but in the kingdom of God (Philippians 3:20). In 1 Peter 2:11, the apostle refers to us as aliens and strangers in this world. He instructs us to abstain from the sinful fleshly lusts, which are personal practices in this culture, but which are foreign to righteous living. On the other hand, regarding civil behavior, scripture instructs Christians to "be subject to the governing authorities" (Romans 13:1, Titus 3:1), and to "submit to every human institution" (1 Peter 2:13). This admonition is consistent throughout the epistles, which were written to churches in different cultures and under varied types of government authority. They were found in Rome, Crete, Ephesus, and scattered throughout Asia Minor. In Romans 13, we are taught that all authority comes from God, and authorities that exist are instituted by God.

> Every person is to be in subjection to the governing authorities. For there is no authority except from God, and those which exist are established by God. Therefore whoever resists authority has opposed the ordinance of God; and they who have opposed will receive condemnation upon themselves. For rulers are not a cause of fear for good behavior, but for evil. Do you want to have no fear of authority? Do what is good and you will have praise from the same; for it is a minister of God to you for good. But if you do what is evil, be afraid; for it does not bear the sword for nothing; for it is a minister of God, an avenger who brings wrath on the one who practices evil. Therefore it is necessary to be in subjection, not only because of wrath, but also for conscience' sake. For because of this you also pay taxes, for rulers are servants of God, devoting themselves to this very thing. Render to all what is due them:

tax to whom tax is due; custom to whom custom; fear to whom fear; honor to whom honor. (Romans 13:1–7)

Even going beyond simple compliance and adherence to laws, we are instructed to pray, intercede, and give thanks for "All men, for kings and all who are in authority," in 1 Timothy 2:1-4. It should be our practice to pray for those in authority, motivated by genuine love and concern for their souls. Praying for those in authority also contributes to our opportunity to "Lead a tranquil and quiet life in all godliness and dignity."

I urge that entreaties and prayers, petitions and thanksgivings, be made on behalf of all men, for kings and all who are in authority, so that we may lead a tranquil and quiet life in all godliness and dignity. This is good and acceptable in the sight of God our Savior, who desires all men to be saved and to come to the knowledge of the truth. (1 Timothy 2:1–4)

Positive interactions should mark your relationships in civic life as you "Keep your behavior excellent among the [world]" (1 Peter 2:12), insofar as it is possible on your part. The instruction we read in Titus 3:1-2 is broad, addressing our relationships with leaders, authorities, and all men. "Remind them to be subject to rulers, to authorities, to be obedient, to be ready for every good deed, to malign no one, to be peaceable, gentle, showing every consideration for all men." This is a portrait of Christ-like humility, as we deny Self and love others, as Christ lives and reigns within us.

UNDERSTANDING THOSE WHO ARE OF THE WORLD

A great challenge for many Christians is knowing how to interact with, or how to respond, when someone in the world expresses views or exhibits behavior or practices which are contrary to righteousness and godly living. Some may ignore that person, as if they were not even present. On the other end of the spectrum, they may feel compelled to react harshly, or in a negative way. Neither of these reactions provides a bridge to an opportunity to share the gospel of Jesus with that person. Ignoring someone can feel dehumanizing (remember, regardless of spiritual status, every person is made in God's image and has a deep-seated need for relationship), and reacting harshly is judgmental.

It is wise to give some thought to how one should expect people without Christ to behave, and to understand why they behave in that manner. In Ephesians 4, Paul writes to the church in Ephesus about those who are not Christians, but instead are in the world:

> So this I say, and affirm together with the Lord, that you walk no longer just as the Gentiles also walk, in the futility of their mind, being darkened in their understanding, excluded from the life of God because of the ignorance that is in them, because of the hardness of their heart; and they, having become callous, have given themselves over to sensuality for the practice of every kind of impurity with greediness. (Ephesians 4:17-19)

When we understand they are "darkened in their understanding" and have become *callous*, we see it is unreasonable to expect them to behave in the same ways as a follower of Jesus. There is no need to judge or respond in disgust toward someone who is acting according to their nature. They may even reject you, or act harshly toward you, because of your faith and testimony of Christ. In 1 Corinthians 2:14, Paul writes, "But a natural man does not accept the things of the Spirit of God, for they are foolishness to him; and he cannot understand them, because they are spiritually appraised." It should never be a surprise if the nonbeliever rejects the message of the gospel. Unless the Holy Spirit gives them ears to hear (faith), the gospel is foolishness to them.

Jesus teaches us that, when we are following Him, we should expect the world to hate us because we are not cut from the same cloth as them. In the same way the world hated Jesus, they will hate us.

> "If the world hates you, you know that it has hated Me before it hated you. If you were of the world, the world would love its own; but because you are not of the world, but I chose you out of the world, because of this the world hates you." (John 15:18–19)

So consider this, that we should expect those in the world to have "given themselves over to sensuality for the practice of every kind of impurity," and that they will hate us just as they hated Christ. Those are the perfect conditions for demonstrating the amazing love of God through our grace-filled responses of kindness and love, despite their offensive behavior and hate. This makes Christians so completely different; we have been literally transformed into new creations in Christ (2 Corinthians 5:17), and it should be noticeable!

DIFFERENT FROM THE WORLD

As *new creatures*, we are unquestionably different from the world.

> Therefore if anyone is in Christ, he is a new creature; the old things passed away; behold, new things have come. Now all these things are from God, who reconciled us to Himself through Christ and gave us the ministry of reconciliation, namely, that God was in Christ reconciling the world to Himself, not counting their trespasses against them, and He has committed to us the word of reconciliation. (2 Corinthians 5:17–19)

The critical tension in our civic and community relationships is that we are called to honor our neighbors of the world and strive to "lead a tranquil and quiet life in all godliness and dignity" (1 Timothy 2:1-4), while refusing to be conformed to the world, as addressed in Romans 12:2. This tension, or conflict, we may feel can be caused by two issues.

First, we may feel tension when we confuse our responsibility to honor all people (1 Peter 2:17) with being conformed to the world. Honoring people who are blatantly sinful is not the same as approving of their sin. This is simplistic thinking and a legalistic rationale. At the heart of this tension is Self, which wants to protect one's reputation and standing in righteousness; Self does not want any association with "those who sin," in fear that such an association would diminish others' views of one's holiness. Self must be denied and placed on the cross, which we take up daily!

Second, when a non-Christian neighbor observes that our behavior differs from theirs (we refuse to engage in lewd talk or behavior, or we are honest in business dealings) they might criticize us for being "holier than thou." We may then feel the tension of wanting to be liked and spoken well of by others. Again, the tension that is felt is Self, who wants to be protected from social harm and persecution. Self must be denied and placed back on the cross, along with the pride that fuels Self. Remember Jesus' words from John 15:18-19, when He said, "If the world hates you, you know that it has hated Me before it hated you. If you were of the world, the world would love its own; but because you are not of the world, but I chose you out of the world, because of this the world hates you."

The difference between the Christian man and the world will be evidenced by his humility in relationship with God and others, and how he prioritizes and values his activities and use of time, his practices and behaviors, and his love for the church (John 13:35). Jesus directs specific practices and behaviors for His followers, which would seem bizarre and confounding to those in the world.

> "You have heard that it was said, 'An eye for an eye, and a tooth for a tooth.' But I say to you, do not resist an evil person; but whoever slaps you on your right cheek, turn the other to him also. If anyone wants to sue you and take your shirt, let him have your coat also. Whoever forces you to go one mile, go with him two. Give to him who asks of you, and do not turn away from him who wants to borrow from you." (Matthew 5:38–42)

A LIGHT FOR THE WORLD

Jesus gives us a clear illustration of how we bring glory to the Father through our testimony of faith and the transformation of our lives, which comes through Christ. He says this in Matthew, chapter five:

> "You are the light of the world. A city set on a hill cannot be hidden; nor does anyone light a lamp and put it under a basket, but on the lampstand, and it gives light to all who are in the house. "Let your light shine before men in such a way that they may see your good works, and glorify your Father who is in heaven." (Matthew 5:14–16)

The light that shines through our lives is not to elevate or bring attention to ourselves, but to cause others to see and glorify the Father.

LOVING THE WORLD

We know that all the disciplines of stewardship grow and develop from, and are motivated by, love for God and love for others. Love for God and love for others is foundational to living as a Christian man. Jesus describes the immensity of this when He says,

> "You have heard that it was said, 'You shall love your neighbor and hate your enemy.' But I say to you, love your enemies and pray for those who persecute you, so that you may be sons of your Father who is in heaven; for He causes His sun to rise on the evil and the good, and sends rain on the righteous and the unrighteous. For if you love those who love you, what reward do you have? Do not even the tax collectors do the same? If you greet only your brothers, what more are you doing than others? Do not even the Gentiles do the same? Therefore you are to be perfect, as your heavenly Father is perfect." (Matthew 5:43–48)

From the world's perspective, it is outlandish to love your enemy! This reveals the scope of differentiation between Christian thought and the world's system of thought. There are many variations of the world's system of thought, but they are all centered on, and driven by, the same thing—Self. Jesus requires the man who wishes to come after Him to deny Self and take up his cross daily. Until the Christian man is obedient to Christ's direction in this, he cannot love his enemy, or pray for those who persecute him. It is only when Christ reigns in the life of a man that he is enabled by the Holy Spirit to love selflessly.

In Luke 10:25-27, Jesus affirms that love of God and love of your neighbor are essential to eternal life. The lawyer then asks Jesus the simple question, "Who is my neighbor?" Jesus replied by telling the parable of the Good Samaritan (Luke 10:30-37). In this story, a Jewish man is traveling, and is robbed and beaten half to death by robbers. As he lay there, two other Jewish travelers came by one at a time, and when they saw the beaten man, they moved to the other side of the road and continued on, without stopping. Finally, a third man, a Samaritan, came along and he felt compassion. He cared for the man's injuries and transported him to an inn, paying for the man's stay at the inn and for further care out of his own pocket. Jesus asked the lawyer, "Which of these three do you think proved to be a neighbor to the man who fell into the robbers' hands?" The lawyer said, "The one who showed mercy toward him." Jesus said to him, "Go and do the same."

What is so significant in this story is that the Jews and the Samaritans hated each other. Jesus makes the point to this Jewish lawyer that it was a *Samaritan* who felt compassion and proved to be a neighbor to the suffering Jewish man, after his own Jewish countrymen had passed by on the other side of the road. The parable actually demonstrates loving those whom the world says should be our enemies.

This is an extraordinary truth, and it provides irrefutable evidence of the transformative impact of the gospel of Jesus Christ. It is when we deny Self and surrender to the reign of Christ in our life, that we are transformed. We are enabled and empowered to love the Lord our God with all our heart, and with all our soul, and with all our mind, and with all our strength, and to love our neighbor as ourself (and even our enemies). In Christ, we are equipped and empowered to fulfill the great commission of Jesus, to "Go therefore and make disciples of all the nations, baptizing them in the name of the Father and the Son and the Holy Spirit, teaching them to observe all that I commanded you; and lo, I am with you always, even to the end of the age." (Matthew 28:19-20)

THE BIG PICTURE

"This really is a big area of stewardship. It encompasses the practice and completion of the great commission of Jesus!" Ethan remarked. "How we discipline our behavior and emotions, in response to government authority and cultural pressures, can be an incredible testimony of the power of Christ transforming our lives, if we actually do it! Not to mention how we respond to people who might despise us for believing and sharing the gospel of Jesus."

"Yes, it is big," Jonathon agreed. "I think it is also one of the best places to test the genuineness of our faith and testimony. There is often a lot of personal fear and apprehension inside a man about any type of public declaration of faith. Then there's not a lot of reinforcement, or positive feedback from the world when a man does step out in obedience. The reinforcement and reward for going out and loving the world and making disciples needs to be grounded firmly in knowing the Father's pleasure in our obedience and the stewardship which He has entrusted to us."

Ethan stared at the table and pondered this for a few moments. Finally he looked up, and softly acknowledged, "Jonathon, I have to confess once again, I could never do this alone. I want to obey God and walk this narrow way of loving people who hate me and caring for people who won't appreciate it. But without you walking with me on this journey, I really don't think I could do it. Denying Self and putting it back on the cross daily is really hard."

"That is true," Jonathon responded with understanding. "I feel the same, Ethan. Every Christian man has a treacherous Self that needs to be crucified. Plus, we are targeted by the world, the devil, and the flesh in the daily battles of life. I really think that may be one reason Jesus always sent His disciples out in pairs to preach about the kingdom of God. He never sent anyone out alone (Luke 10:1-11).

"Ethan, this narrow way is meant to be walked together; that is how God designed and created us to function. We need to be encouraged and strengthened by one another as we walk this narrow and difficult way. Together, we grow in our understanding and celebrate the reign of Christ within us, and we walk humbly with God each day."

Discussion and Discipline

- Government authority, on the federal, state, and local level, plays a significant role in the life of every man by setting restrictions, limiting behavior, and requiring payments (taxes). It is not surprising to feel conflicted about being told what to do. As a Christian, how do you handle yourself when you disagree with the "heavy hand" of government? Are you able to submit without complaining or bitterness, keeping "your behavior excellent among the [world]" (1 Peter 2:12)? What is the first step in learning to practice this?

- Have you made it a practice to pray, intercede, and give thanks for those in authority (1 Timothy 2:1-4)? If you've disciplined yourself in this practice, do you think it might reduce the irritation you may at times feel about government restrictions on you?

- If we understand that those in the world are darkened in their understanding, does it make it easier not to judge them for sinful behavior (Ephesians 4:17-19)? Might you even be able to feel compassion for them as they walk in darkness? Knowing that Jesus said we should expect the world to hate us, why should we ever be surprised if we are mistreated by those in the world?

- Some Christians feel compelled to be Self-protective as they relate to those in the world. They don't want to stand out and seem "weird" to others. What do you think is the problem with this perspective as a follower of Jesus? Is it contrary to Jesus' declaration that Christians are "the light of the world" (Matthew 5:14-16)?

- The practice of loving the world does not come naturally for men. It is a discipline that needs to be practiced, a stewardship from the Father that needs to be honored and put to use, just as the Good Samaritan cared for and provided medical treatment for his natural enemy. How might it turn your world upside down to shock your "enemy" by showing kindness and care for them? What person comes to your mind that would fit that category, for whom you can plan to love? What action will you take to do that?

MAPPING THE JOURNEY

JOURNEY

The Narrow Way

DDS

DDS PUBLISHING

DDS Publishing

Chapter Eighteen

Men Walking With God

Steps Along the Way

Ours is a world which caters to the fickle demands of Self and tantalizes the lust of the flesh, the lust of the eyes, and the boastful pride of life. The appeal to Self is bold in the daily barrage of commercial advertisements. Vintage Burger King advertising in the 1970s told the consumer to, "Have it your way!" This evolved over the years until 2022, when the new declaration was, "You rule!" The broad appeal of this mantra in society may even lead to the formation of an imitation christian life and church. In this imitation, Self reigns within each individual and the goal for programs is to ensure everyone involved can "have it their way." This is a wide gate and a broad way that is inviting, entertaining, easy, and leads to destruction (Matthew 7:13).

The same Jesus who overturned the tables of the money changers in the temple disrupts and overturns the foundations and logic of sin-corrupted mankind. He declares that God's plan for salvation is a small gate and a narrow way that leads to life (Matthew 7:14). Salvation is *very* narrow. It is by grace alone, through faith alone, and in Christ alone! There are few who find this narrow way.

DENY SELF

If you want to join Jesus, you must deny your Self, and take up your cross daily and follow Him (Luke 9:23-24). Self can no longer be allowed to reign over your life. It must be crucified (put to death) daily. This is incredibly offensive to the world, but it is life-giving to the Christian (Luke 9:24)!

For the word of the cross is foolishness to those who are perishing, but to us who are being saved it is the power of God. (1 Corinthians 1:18)

RECEIVE THE KINGDOM (REIGN) OF GOD LIKE A CHILD

Humility of heart and mind is the key which opens the door to receiving the reign of God within you. Humility germinates with denying Self, and blossoms with the recognition and acknowledgement that God is everything, and as His creation, you are empty of significance without Him. Receiving the reign of God like a child (in humility) is the restoration of created man's natural relationship with God and begins the glorious journey of walking humbly with Him.

SPIRITUAL WARFARE

As we walk on this narrow way with God, we are transformed by the renewing of our mind. This happens when the truth of His Word shines light on the fortresses of speculation in our mind that are raised up against the knowledge of God. Those fortresses are destroyed as we take every thought captive to the obedience of Christ (1 Corinthians 10:5). The daily disciplines of reading the Bible, praying at all times, and worship equip us for this battle. The mind renewed by the Word of God dwells on things that are true, honorable, right, pure, lovely, things of good repute, excellent things, and things worthy of praise (Philippians 4:8).

STEWARDSHIP

God designed us to be His stewards of creation. Now, restored to right relationship with Him, we learn through His word to be faithful, fruitful, and generous stewards of our gracious Master. There is no greater joy nor significance than to be and to work as God designed for us to live. Each day we have significant purpose as we love and serve our Master, faithfully stewarding the resources, gifts, and time He has entrusted to us on our stewardship journey.

FINISHING THE JOURNEY

Jesus describes the scene at the culmination of our journey along the narrow way. Only then will we see clearly and fully realize the extent to which we have been walking with God each day. Jesus explains,

> "But when the Son of Man comes in His glory, and all the angels with Him, then He will sit on His glorious throne. All the nations will be gathered before Him; and He will separate them from one another, as the shepherd separates the sheep from the goats; and He will put the sheep on His right, and the goats on the left. Then the King will say to those on His right, 'Come, you who are blessed of My Father, inherit the kingdom prepared for you from the foundation of the world. For I was hungry, and you gave Me something to eat; I was thirsty, and you gave Me something to drink; I was a stranger, and you invited Me in; naked, and you clothed Me; I was sick, and you visited Me; I was in prison, and you came to Me.'
>
> Then the righteous will answer Him, 'Lord, when did we see You hungry, and feed You, or thirsty, and give You something to drink? And when did we see You a stranger, and invite You in, or naked, and clothe You? When did we see You sick, or in prison, and come to You?'
>
> **The King will answer and say to them, 'Truly I say to you, to the extent that you did it to one of these brothers of Mine, even the least of them, you did it to Me.'"** (Matthew 25:31–40)

Acknowledgements

I am beyond thankful to my amazing wife, Linda. You supported and encouraged me through the writing process and patiently viewed endless home improvement shows solo in the living room while I pounded on the keyboard in the office. Your frank and insightful feedback moved me back onto the right path many times. You are my beautiful Gem—my greatest treasure!

I am so grateful for my brother-in-law, Pastor Marc Farschman, who scrutinized and weighed each page, sentence, and word of an early draft. You were clear and full of praise for the truth you saw, and bold and fearless in pointing out naked emperors. There are many <u>fewer</u> 40-word sentences because of your diligence!

Thank you, Pastor David Foss, for your critical feedback on the content. An entire section within Personal Stewardship would be missing without your keen observation. Thank you for wrestling through some of the theology with me—I love these discussions with you!

To my lifelong friend and coworker in Christ, Pastor Kevin McClure, I greatly appreciate your humility and transparency as we talked through your review and feedback on the book. Thank you!

My heartfelt "Thank you!" is insufficient to express my gratitude to my sister, Marlys Hamilton. You poured your time and expertise into hundreds and hundreds of edits and corrections on formatting, grammar, and punctuation. You have an amazing eye for detail!